GLIMPSES OF RENEWABLE ENERGY

Renewable Energy Technology

Dr R P Gupta

Clever Fox® PUBLISHING
Chennai • Bangalore

CLEVER FOX PUBLISHING
Chennai, India

Published by CLEVER FOX PUBLISHING 2025

ISBN: 978-93-6707-498-5

DEDICATED TO MY BELOVED WIFE ANITA WHO LEFT US FOR HEVEANILY ABODE ON 10TH JANUARY 2025

(1962-2025)

FOREWORD

NEERAJ SINHA

It is a privilege and a pleasure to write the Foreword to this insightful and timely book on solar energy as applicable to India, authored by my friend and colleague, Dr. R. P. Gupta.

In an era where the urgency to transition to clean, sustainable sources of energy is no longer a matter of debate but of action, solar power stands out as one of the most promising solutions—especially for a country like India. With its vast geographic diversity and abundant sunlight throughout the year, India holds immense untapped potential in solar energy. This book not only explores that potential but also provides a grounded understanding of the technological, economic, environmental, and policy dimensions shaping the sector.

What makes this book particularly valuable is its clarity, relevance, and commitment to real-world applicability. It bridges the gap between academic insight and practical implementation. Whether you are a student, a policymaker, a technologist, or simply someone interested in India's energy future, you will find this work informative, thought-provoking, and inspiring.

Dr. R. P. Gupta brings to this subject a rare combination of deep technical knowledge and an unwavering commitment to sustainability. Through this book, he presents a compelling case for why solar energy is not just a technological option but a national imperative for India—an imperative that promises energy security, economic resilience, and environmental stewardship.

I am confident that this book will serve as a valuable guide and reference for many, and will contribute meaningfully to the growing discourse on renewable energy in India, *more so in view of the country's target to achieve net zero carbon emissions by the year 2030.*

Adviser

Office of the Principle Advise to the Government of India

Cabinet Secretariat

Vigyan Bhawan Annexe

Maulana Azad Road

Delhi 110011

FOREWORD

ABOUT NEERAJ SINHA

Dr Sinha has a background in Mechanical Engineering and has over 25 years of experience working in scientific organizations of the Government of India. In his role at the Office of the Principal Scientific Adviser, he has been involved in a wide range of scientific activities including:

* Oil Spill Management
* Underground Coal Gasification
* Technologically Important Crystals
* Bulk Encryption
* Explosive Detection
* Integrated Gasification Combined Cycle for Coal-based Power Generation * Night Vision Devices
* Setting up of a National Knowledge Network
* Multipurpose National Identity Cards

He also actively contributed to the preparation of the National Action Plan on Climate Change, which was released by the Prime Minister of India on June 30, 2008. He has submitted a thesis on "III-Nitrides for energy related (Photovoltaic and LED) applications" for his Ph.D. degree and has co-authored over 20 scientific papers on this subject. He is a life Member of the Institution of Engineers (India) and the Administrative Staff College of India, Hyderabad.

Prior to this role, Dr. Neeraj Sinha was a Senior Adviser at NITI Aayog. He was relieved from his duties there on January 17, 2024, to join his current office.

CONTENTS

CHAPTER 1

RURAL ENERGY SCENARIO OF INDIA

The rural energy sector in India has undergone significant transformation in recent years. There's been a shift towards universal access to electricity and the adoption of cleaner fuels. However, challenges persist, particularly concerning the quality and reliability of supply, affordability, and the ability to transition to clean cooking solutions.

Detailed Look at Rural Energy Sector in India:

1. Electricity Access and Supply - Significant Progress:

* Near-universal electrification: India has made remarkable strides in rural electrification. As of March 2022, all villages were reportedly electrified under the Saubhagya *scheme*, connecting over 2.86 crore households. Overall, electricity access in India has risen to 99.6% (by 2022), up from 80% in 2000.
* Improved Power Supply Duration: The availability of rural power supply has

Increased in rural areas. significantly increased from 12.5 kWh in 2015 to 29.5 kWh in 2024

Reduced energy shortage: The gap between energy requirements and energy supplied has drastically reduced from 9.7% in 2013-14 to 0.1% in FY 24-25 .

Persistent Gaps: Despite high electrification ratio, a small percentage of households particularly The poorest the rural households still has access to electricity (about 18% poorest rural households in 2023). Furthermore, while connections are wide spread, the quality and reliability of power such as issues like intermittent supply, low voltage and frequent outages remain critical challenges, specially in rural region

Rural Micro enterprises: Many rural micro enterprises still lack grid connections and rely on diesel generators, indicating a significant unmet demand for reliable and affordable energy for productive uses.

Government Schemes and Initiatives

Content

Govt has launched various schemes to bolster rural energy access and promote renewable energy access and promote renewable energy.

Deen Dayal Upadhyaya Gram Jyoti Yojana (DDUGJY):

This scheme focused on electrification, un-electrified villages and strengthening sub-transmission and distribution networks in rural areas and electrified 18,374 villages.

* Saubhagya Scheme (Pradhan Mantri Sahaj Bijli Har Ghar Yojana)

Aimed at electrifying all willing un-electrified households in rural areas and urban areas both.

DDUGJY and Saubhagya schemes closed in March 2022.

* Reformed Revamped Distribution Sector Scheme (RDSS):
* Launched with an outlay of Rs. 3,03,759 (approx) crore. This scheme aims to improve the operation and financial sustainability of distribution companies (DISCOMs).
* It provides financial assistance for infrastructure upgradation, including new HT and LT lines.
* Key focus areas:
* Feeder segregation.
* New/Augmentation of distribution transformers.

And creating Creation of resilient distribution infrastructure."

* "Deen Dayal Upadhyaya Gram Jyoti Yojana (DDUGJY)" This is a known rural electrification scheme in India

"Saubhagya - A scheme launched to provide free electricity to households.

This refers to the Pradhan Mantri Sahaj Bijli Har Ghar Yojana, also known as Saubhagya, for household electrification.

Target:

To provide free electricity to households through rooftop solar installations, 25 kilowatts 4 lakh, 100 rooftop solar installation

* "Pradhan Mantri Kisan Urja Suraksha Utthan Mahabhiyan (PM-KUSUM Scheme)" (This is a significant scheme in India aimed at providing financial and water security to farmers by encouraging the use of solar energy for irrigation.)
* "Gramin Vidyutikaran Niti (Rural Electrification Policy)" (This is a general policy framework.)

* "Under this scheme, subsidies for farmers to install solar irrigation pumps for cultivation within can farmer eligible." (This details a benefit under one of the mentioned scheme PM-KUSUM:
* In conclusion rural energy has been on a good trajectory."
* "It aims towards sustainable and equitable energy access."
* "While significant achievements have been made in electrification, the focus is to increase supply."
* "Improved energy quality
* "On affordability and the integration of renewable energy solutions to empower rural economies." "And improve the quality of life." "Address the remaining challenges."

Through innovative financing models Accountability engagement and robust implementation Development will be crucial for achieving vision of Developed India 2047."

"Rural energy Sector of India Problems and issues."

"Rural India's energy structure Issues -

* "Defining the rural energy structure in India outlining its key components including grid connectivity and the gap of traditional energy sources.
* "Analyzing the current status of rural energy access and consumption patterns across different regions of India highlighting disparities."

The infrastructural problems with in the rural energy structure such as grid reliability, transmission and distribution losses and last mile connectivity challenges."

* "And identification economic and financial issues implying Rural Energy Structures include affordably for consumers, cost recovery for utilities and access to finance for inform a structure development."

* A sub-point policy Regulatory"

*: "Key problems and ISSUES in Indian Rural Energy Sector:
* "Infrastructure Gaps and Last mile Connectivity"
* "Incomplete Coverage: While India has achieved high levels of household electrification, a small percentage of small households particularly in remote and difficult terrain remain un electrified. This section include newly formed households or those that have fallen into poverty since earlier datasets were compiled."
* "Grid Reliability and Quality: Even in electrified areas, rural homes and businesses frequently frequently experienced unscheduled power cuts, low voltage and frequent interruption. This unreliable supply hinders economic activity and diminishes consumer satisfaction."

High (T&D Losses):

India faces significant T&D losses around 15-8%, in 2022-23 much higher than the global average. This leads to wasted electricity and revenue losses for distribution companies (Discoms).

* Financial Losses & Constraints and affordability:
* Financial Distress of Discoms: State Power Distribution Companies are often financially due to huge accumulated losses (e.g., lack of timely recovery (especially in rural areas with subsidized tariffs) and poor collection rates. This limits their ability to invest in infrastructure upgrades and ensure consistent service.
* High upfront cost of Renewable Energy: While beneficial in long run, the initial capital investment is especially substantial. Setting up of Solar Power plants and other renewable energy systems is often prohibitive for communities with limited financial resources.
* Inadequate subsidies
* High dependent on imports

Grid Integration Issues

* Lack of awareness of skilled work force
* Socio-Economic Impact on Rehabilitation Aspects
* Social challenges in energy survey, rural area data
* The impact of unreliable data on rural energy planning and data.
* Informal Energy Sources data gaps -

In many Indian data reliability and scarcity are significant challenges in collecting data and planning for the data in micro-level energy sector.

* Outdated and official data sets for energy permits might not be based on real data.
* Energy production and impact Energy Consumption.
* Biomass (Firewood, crop residue, cow dung)

Consumption Data" and "challenges in survey methodology." There's also a point about improving "robust energy services" and data sharing.

Rural Energy

* Scope of rural energy: Refers to sources and uses of energy in rural areas, including
* Access to electricity
* The percentage of rural households or population that has access to electricity.
* Sources of Energy: The types of traditional and technologies used by rural households for various uses (cooking, lighting, and heating, etc.).
* Consumption patterns: How much energy is consumed in rural areas and for what purposes (Residential, Agricultural, Commercial).
* India as a significant country: India is highlighted as a significant country with a large population and active efforts in rural energy development.

* Access to Electricity in rural areas: Mentions that India has made remarkable progress in rural electrification.

As of 2023, 99.2% of rural population had access to electricity across the world.

* Indian Households with LPG (2023): "In 2023, nearly 97% of India households were electrified with 96.7% [likely LPG] connections."
* Cooking Fuel: "Relying on LPG as primary cooking fuel is only 26% in rural areas like Uttar Pradesh, Rajasthan, Haryana, and Bihar." (This highlights a disparity in LPG adoption despite high connection rates, suggesting continued reliance on traditional fuels).
* Average Power Supply in Rural Areas: "The average availability of power supply in rural areas (in hours) increased from 12.5 hours in 2015 to 21.9 hours in 2024."

Conclusions

Rural energy has been on a good trajectory.It aims towards sustainable and equitable energy access.

* While significant achievements have been made in electrification, the focus is to increase supply.
* <u>Improved energy quality</u>
* "On affordability and the integration of renewable energy solutions to empower rural economies." and improve the quality of life." "Address the remaining challenges."

Through innovative financing models Accountability engagement and robust implementation Development will be crucial for achieving vision of Developed India 2047."

References:

1. "Sustainable Energy without hot Paid J.C. Mackay"
2. "Introduction to Renewable Energy Vaughan, Nelson and 140 moth L.""Stanford"
3. "General Renewable Energy Journal"
4. "Energy for Sustainable Development"

*5. Energies (MDPI) mm

*6. Ministry of New and Renewable Energy Annual Reports,2021-22,2022-23,2023-24,2024-25

CHAPTER 2

ASSESSMENT OF RENEWABLE ENERGY PROGRAMME IN INDIA

Introduction

India's renewable energy sector is experiencing remarkable boom driven by ambitious government targets, declining technology costs and increasing environmental awareness. It is a critical component of India's commitment to combat climate change and ensure energy security.clean energy rankings in solar wind and overall renewable energy based on recent data."

India has made remarkable strides in solar energy and holds a significant global position. According to recent Reports from 2023 data3rd largest solar market for additions, India was 3rd largest market globally for solar capacity additions 2024.Only a record 281.63 GW of solar capacity. This places only behind China and the United States.

Renewable Energy Contribution to GD P

Significance of Renewable Energy: "The renewable energy sector is playing an increasingly significant role in India's GDP, economic growth through various channels, with a specific percentage contribution for GDP in a specific year can be found based on market methodology of calculating how we measure the impact and its contributions.

Direct and Indirect Contribution to GDP:

Investment and Growth: "India has witnessed a rapid growth in renewable energy investments. But 2023 clean energy contributed slightly less than 3% of India's GDP growth, primarily driven by investments in new solar power capacity.

Clean Energy Investment Growth:

Clean energy investments reached USD 68 billion in 2023, nearly 40% higher than 2016-2020 average. This investment fuels economic activity through manufacturing and development of renewable energy projects.

Job creation:

The renewable energy sector is highly labor-intensive, generating millions of jobs. Cross-sector segments include manufacturing, installation, operations, maintenance, and research and development. It's mentioned that the solar PV sector alone supplied about 3,18,500 jobs, and the wind sector provided approximately 52,200 jobs. This directly and indirectly boosts household incomes and stimulates the economy.

Reduced import bill: By increasing domestic energy output from renewable sources, India reduces its reliance on imported fossil fuels like oil and coal. This significantly lowered the country's energy import bill, which was about 3.1% of GDP, thereby improving trade balance and saving valuable foreign exchange.

Industrial growth and manufacturing.

Significant Growth in installed capacity (FY 2020-21 & FY 2024-25) Overall RE Capacity: India has demonstrated robust growth in its renewable energy capacity. As of March 31 2025, the total installed renewable capacity reached 220 GW, a significant increase from 198 GW in previous fiscal year. This includes large hydro.

* *Capacity addition FY 2024-25 saw a capacity addition of 24 GW in RE Sector.*

Solar Power Dominance:

Solar energy remains the leading contributor to growth .

* FY 2023-24:
* 23.83 GW of new solar capacity was added. The total installed capacity rose to 105.6 GW, including ground-mounted, rooftop, hybrid, and off-grid solar projects
* FY 2022-23 Approximately 10.03 GW of solar capacity was added.

* **Wind Power Progress**:

Wind energy also saw sustained growth

* FY 2023-24:

4.15 GW of new wind capacity was added, resulting in a total cumulative intake with

capacity of 50.0046 GW.

* FY 2022-23

: 3.24 GW of wind capacity was added.

* **Other Renewable Sources:**

* Bioenergy:Total capacity reached 11.58 GW, including biomass and waste-to-energy.
* Small Hydropower:

Contributed a capacity of 5.06 GW, with another 0.44 GW under implementation.

Global Energy

* Renewable Energy installed capacity.
* Solar Power

Capacity 4 GW in wind and 5 GW in solar power capacity.

* **Green Hydrogen:**
* National Green Hydrogen Mission

With an allocated budget (e.g., 600 crore to FY2024).

* Establishment of Hydrogen Production Hubs.

Present Status:

* Tenders and Awards: For green hydrogen production.
* Financial Incentives: For manufacturing electrolyzers and components.
* Production Targets: Aiming for 5 MM tonnes of green hydrogen by 2030.
* **"PM KUSUM" scheme**:

Relates to solar pumps for agricultural use.

The overall content suggests a discussion of a country's (likely India's) policies, targets, and progress in renewable energy, with a particular emphasis on green hydrogen nationwide by Dec 2024 (Capacity to 330 by Dec 2024)" refers to a target for nationwide energy capacity.135 lakh micro connect agriculture proposed solareged - Suggests a proposal for solarizing agricultural micro-connect Achievements

* "over 4 lakh farmers has benefiting till Feb 2024" - Indicates the number of farmers who have benefited from a scheme.

* "**PM Suryagarh Muft Bijali Yojana**

launched in 2024 this scheme has significantly boost up top solar installater" - Refers to the launch of a solar energy scheme (PM Suryagarh Muft Bijali Yojana) in 2024 and its positive impact on solar installation work in 10 months" - installation work progress.

* "Solar Park: As of November 2023, 50 to Solar Park with an aggregate capacity of around 37.490 MW were approved across 12 states. 19401 MW of solar projects

have been commissioning work in these park" - data on approved and commissioned solar parks in India as of November 2023.

* "Budget targets: MNRE aims to issue for 50GW per annum of RE capacity for with at least 10GW/Annual power from 2023-24 (so to work issues): FY2023-24 (till Dec 23)" - Details the Ministry of New and Renewable Energy (MNRE)'s annual targets for renewable energy (RE) capacity.

* "IREDA Upgrade: Indian Renewable Energy was upgrade as schedule A Category PSUE- it is instruments of AA+ rating rating financial strong strong of RR project - the upgrade of IREDA (Indian Renewable Energy Development Agency) to a Schedule A Public Sector Enterprise (PSE) and its AA+ rating, indicating financial strength.

Biomass Promotion: Revised Policy

* Financial Assistance (CFAM): To boost manufacturing plants, - consultants and outreach.
* Policy Simplification - MNRE: policy review and simplifying guidelines to ensure implementation, and promotion of better quality installations.
* 500 GW Non-Fossil Fuel Capacity by 2023: Indicates a target for non-fossil fuel energy.
* Achieving 500 GW of Non-Fossil Fuel Energy Capacity by 2023: Reiterates the target and mentions "a commitment to whole the planet."
* Renewable Purchase Obligation (RPO):

States

A target by2024 of 29.% of total energy must come from renewable sources" and a gradual increase to 43%

* Separate RPO for Dealer-based Renewable Energy (DRE): a distinct policy for renewable energy generated by dealers.
* Green Hydrogen Policy: Indicates an "upcoming policy" or principles related to green hydrogen to reduce grey all raps investment and establish as MNRE as global hub"

Manufacturing: Expansion: scale up domestic Solar PV and wind turbines

manufacturing to double share of on India to become a global RE manufacturing hub" (RE likely stands for Renewable Energy)

* "Grand Infrastructure Development :significant investment system to evacuate pure power from renewable rich state Pvt. : Allocation of budgetary outlay for existing infrastructure for hydro electric projects (HEP) with a total outlay 12,461 crore. FY 2025to2030 outlay

Addressing Problems and Issues

Land acquisition: Delays in land acquisition led to late stage projects and hinder the progress.

* Clearances:Streamline environmental & other regulatory clearances (time bound)
* Grid Integration: Ensuring robust grid infrastructure to evacuate and integrate

renewable energy assets and ensure energy.

* Storage solutions:
* Developing cost effective energy storage solutions addresses the intermittency of solar and wind power.
* Financial Viability: Ensuring financial mechanisms to develop and invest especially for emerging technologies.
* Skill:
* Development, building & skilled workforce to support the rapid expansion of the renewable energy sector.

Salient features of Renewable Energy Sector: Emphasizes its potential for labor intensive job creation, particularly in manufacturing, installation, operations, maintenance, and research and development.

* Job Creation Numbers: States that in 2023, the solar PV sector supplied about 3,18,600 jobs and the wind sector provided approximately 52,200 jobs.

* Economic Impact: Notes that this workforce employment boosts household incomes and stimulates economic demand.
* Reduced Import Bill: Highlights that increasing domestic energy production from renewable sources can reduce reliance on imported fossil fuels like oil and coal. This significantly lowers the country's energy import bill (which was about 3% of GDP), thereby improving its trade balance and saving foreign exchange.

* Industrial Growth and Manufacturing

Experts: India will need to invest nearly 10% of GDP annually (from private & public) from each year over next decade to expand and upgrade its electricity and gas to meet demand & energy targets 2032 Energy sector," largely synonymous with renewable energy and the broader energy transition, faces a complex array of problems and issues as it strives to replace traditional fossil fuels and meet growing global energy demand. These challenges span technological, infrastructural, economic, political, and social dimensions.

Here are some of the key problems and issues:

1. Intermittency Challenges

* Intermittency: Solar and wind power, the leading renewable sources, are by nature intermittent – they only generate electricity when the sun shines or the wind blows.

This variability creates challenges for grid stability and reliable supply, as energy demand is constant.

* Energy Storage: The lack of affordable, scalable, and efficient energy storage solutions (like large-scale batteries, pumped hydro, or green hydrogen) is a major bottleneck. While battery costs are decreasing, current technologies are not yet sufficient to store vast amounts of renewable energy for extended periods, especially for grid-scale applications.
* Balancing Supply and Demand: Without robust storage, managing the fluctuating output of renewals to match real-time demand is a complex operational challenge for grid operators.
* 2. Grid Infrastructure and IntegrationAging Grid: Much of the existing electricity grid infrastructure globally was designed for centralized, fossil fuel-based power plants. It is often old, inflexible, and not capable of efficiently handling large amounts of distributed and variable renewable energy.
* Transmission Bottlenecks: Renewable energy sources are often located in remote areas (e.g., windy plains, sunny deserts, offshore wind farms) far from population centers where demand is highest. Building new transmission lines faces significant challenges, including land acquisition, environmental concerns, and "Not In My Backyard" (NIMBY) opposition.
* Grid Modernization and Digitization: Integrating renewables requires a "smarter" grid with advanced sensors, digital controls, and AI to manage complex power flows, predict demand, and optimize supply. This modernization requires substantial investment and technological upgrades.
* Grid Stability and Resilience: Integrating variable renewables can impact grid inertia and stability, potentially leading to frequency and voltage issues.

Technologies like grid-forming inverters and flexible loads are needed to address this.

3. Supply Chain Vulnerabilities and Raw Material Constraints

* Critical Mineral Dependence: Clean energy technologies (solar panels, wind turbines, EV batteries) are highly dependent on specific critical minerals like lithium, cobalt, nickel, rare earth elements, copper, and graphite. The extraction and processing of many of these minerals are concentrated in a few countries (e.g., China for rare earths, Democratic Republic of Congo for cobalt), creating geopolitical risks and supply chain vulnerabilities.

* Resource Scarcity and Price Volatility: Increased demand for these minerals can lead to price spikes and potential shortages, impacting the cost and speed of the energy transition.

* Ethical Sourcing: Concerns exist about the environmental and social impacts of mining these critical minerals, including child labor, poor working conditions, and environmental degradation, leading to calls for more ethical and sustainable sourcing.

* Manufacturing Capacity: While manufacturing capacity for components like solar panels has expanded rapidly, there are still bottlenecks and geographical imbalances in the global supply chain, particularly for advanced components and energy storage.

4. Economic and Financial Challenges

* High Upfront Costs: While the operational costs of renewables are low, the initial capital investment for large-scale renewable projects (e.g., offshore wind farms, large solar parks, battery storage facilities) can be substantial.

* Financing Risks: Renewable energy projects often face higher perceived risks for investors due to policy uncertainty, grid integration challenges, and market fluctuations. Securing low-cost financing can be difficult, especially in developing economies.

* Market Design: Existing electricity markets were often designed for dispatchable fossil fuel power. Adapting these markets to properly value and incentivize variable renewable energy, flexibility, and storage services is an ongoing challenge.

* Subsidies and Policy Uncertainty: While subsidies have driven renewable deployment, inconsistent or unpredictable government policies, changes in incentives, and administrative barriers can deter investment and slow project development.Cost of Transition: The overall cost of transitioning from a fossil fuel-based economy to a clean energy one involves not just new investments but also managing the retirement of existing fossil fuel assets and ensuring a just transition for workers and communities dependent on these industries.

5. Policy, Regulatory, and Permitting Hurdles

* Regulatory Complexity: Navigating complex and often outdated regulatory frameworks for renewable energy projects, grid connections, and land use can lead to significant delays and increased costs.
* Lengthy Permitting Processes: Obtaining permits for new power plants, transmission lines, and energy storage facilities can take years, slowing down deployment.
* Lack of Long-Term Vision: A clear, stable, and long-term policy vision is often missing, leading to uncertainty for investors and developers.

* Inter-State/Regional Coordination: In many countries, disparate policies and regulations across different states or regions can hinder large-scale renewable energy development and grid integration.

6. Social and Environmental Concerns

* Public Acceptance (NIMBY): While public support for renewable energy in general is high, specific projects (wind farms, solar farms, transmission lines) often face local opposition due to concerns about visual impact, noise, land use, and environmental effects (e.g., impact on birds for wind turbines, habitat disruption for large solar farms).
* Land Use: Large-scale renewable energy projects require significant land area, which can lead to conflicts with agriculture, conservation efforts, and local communities.
* Environmental Footprint of Manufacturing: While renewables reduce operational emissions, the manufacturing of components involves resource extraction, processing, and transportation, which have their own environmental footprints.
* Waste Management: Managing end-of-life solar panels, wind turbine blades, and EV batteries requires robust recycling infrastructure to prevent new waste streams.

7. Human Capital and Workforce Development

* Skills Gap: The rapid growth of the new energy sector requires a skilled workforce for manufacturing, installation, operation, and maintenance of renewable energy technologies. There's often a shortage of adequately trained personnel.
* Job Transition: Ensuring that workers in the fossil fuel industry have opportunities to transition to new jobs in the clean energy sector is a critical social and economic challenge.

Addressing these interconnected issues requires a concerted effort from governments, industry, researchers, and communities to accelerate the global energy transition while ensuring energy security Acknowledgments: Acknowledgements are due to Dr Yash Pal Singh for his kind inspiration and guidance.

References:

1. International Renewable Energy Agency (irena.org)
2. Ministry of New and Renewable Energy -Annual Reports 2024-25,2023-24,2022-23, 2021-22(mnre.gov,in)
3. Ember(ember-energy.org)
4. PIB official press releases (pib.gov.in)
5. IER(Renewable Reports and data)(iea.org)

CHAPTER 3

SOLAR ENERGY PROGRAMME IN INDIA CHINA AND DENMARK AND IMPACT ON SOCIETY, ENVIRONMENT AAD CLIMATE MITIGATION

I
INTRODUCTION

India has emerged as a global leader in solar energy, with ambitious targets and significant achievements in its solar energy program. The country's commitment to clean energy is a crucial part of its National Action Plan on Climate Change and its pledge to achieve net-zero emissions by 2070.

India and Denmark have a strong and growing partnership in the energy sector, particularly focusing on renewable energy, including solar power. This collaboration is primarily driven by their "Green Strategic Partnership."

Here's a breakdown of their solar energy program and broader energy cooperation

* Renewed Memorandum of Understanding (MoU): India and Denmark recently (May 2025) renewed their energy cooperation MoU, which was originally signed in June 2020. This renewal ensures continuity and expands the scope of their collaboration.

Focus on Clean and Sustainable Energy Solutions: The renewed MoU emphasizes knowledge exchange and technological collaboration, particularly in clean and sustainable energy solutions, which includes solar power India and China stand out as the two biggest players in the global solar energy landscape, but their approaches, strengths, and roles differ significantly. While both are committed to massive solar expansion to meet energy demands and climate goals, China leads in sheer scale and manufacturing dominance, while India is rapidly catching up in deployment and focusing on building domestic capabilities.

Key Initiatives and Schemes: in India

India's solar energy program is driven by several government schemes and policies, primarily overseen by the Ministry of New and Renewable Energy (MNRE). Some of the major initiatives include:

* **Jawaharlal Nehru National Solar Mission (JNNSM): Launched in 2010, this mission aimed to establish India as a global leader in solar energy. Initially targeting 20,000 MW by 2022, this target was significantly revised to 100,000 MW (100 GW) by 2022, which India largely achieved.**
* PM Surya Ghar: Muft Bijli Yojana: Launched in February 2024, this scheme aims to increase rooftop solar capacity and provide free electricity to households. It offers substantial subsidies (up to 60% for systems up to 2kW and 40% for 2- 3kW systems) for installing solar panels on residential rooftops. The scheme targets 1 crore (10 million) households and has an outlay of Rs 75,021 crore.
* PM-KUSUM Scheme (Pradhan Mantri Kisan Urja Suraksha evam Utthaan Mahabhiyan): This scheme, launched in 2019, focuses on solarizing agricultural practices. It includes setting up decentralized solar power plants on farmers' land, installing standalone solar pumps, and solarizing grid-connected agricultural pumps. Farmers receive significant financial assistance under this scheme.
* Solar Park Scheme: This scheme provides financial support to establish large-scale solar parks (generally 500 MW and above) to facilitate infrastructure development like land, transmission, and water access for solar power projects.
* Grid Connected Rooftop Solar Programme: This program offers Central Financial Assistance (CFA) for rooftop solar installations, encouraging both residential and commercial sectors to adopt solar power.
* Production Linked Incentive (PLI) Scheme for High Efficiency Solar PV Modules: This scheme aims to boost domestic manufacturing of solar PV modules, making India a global renewable energy manufacturing hub.

Targets and Achievements:

* India has set an ambitious goal of achieving 500 GW of non-fossil fuel-based energy capacity by 2030. Solar energy is expected to contribute nearly 300 GW to this target.
* As of February 28, 2025, India's installed solar capacity stood at approximately 102.57 GW.
* In 2024, India added a record-breaking 24.5 GW of solar capacity, more than double the installations in 2023. This included 18.5 GW of utility-scale solar and 4.59 GW of rooftop solar.

* States like Rajasthan, Gujarat, and Tamil Nadu have been at the forefront of solar energy development.
* India is home to some of the world's largest solar parks, including the Bhadla Solar Park in Rajasthan. The Gujarat Hybrid Renewable Energy Park, when completed, will be the world's largest hybrid renewable energy park.

Impact of Solar Energy Programs:

* Environmental Benefits: Solar energy is a clean and sustainable alternative to fossil fuels, significantly reducing greenhouse gas emissions and air pollution.
* Energy Security: By reducing reliance on imported fossil fuels, solar energy enhances India's energy security and reduces exposure to price volatility.
* Job Creation: The solar energy sector has generated thousands of direct and indirect jobs in manufacturing, installation, maintenance, and research.
* Rural Electrification: Decentralized solar power solutions have played a crucial role in bringing electricity to remote and off-grid areas, improving living standards and enabling economic activities.
* Reduced Energy Costs: The decreasing cost of solar panels and increased efficiency have made solar energy more affordable for households and industries, leading to lower energy expenses.
* Economic Growth: The sector has attracted substantial investment, including significant Foreign Direct Investment (FDI), and contributes to the "Make in India" in

CHALANGES

land acquisition issues for large-scale projects, grid integration challenges, financing constraints, and the need for a skilled workforce. However, with continued government support, technological advancements, and increasing private investment, India's solar energy program is poised for further exponential growth.

An overview of its current status and key initiatives:

Current Status and Achievements (as of May 2025):

* Significant Installed Capacity: India's cumulative solar power capacity has reached 110.83 GW as of May 31, 2025. This includes:
* Ground Mounted Solar Plants: 84.43 GW
* Grid Connected Solar Rooftop: 18.37 GW
* Hybrid Projects (Solar Component): 3.02 GW
* Off-Grid Solar: 5.01 GW

* Rapid Growth: Solar energy continues to be the largest contributor to India's renewable energy capacity expansion. In the Financial Year 2024-25, India added a remarkable 23.83 GW of solar capacity.
* Leading States: Rajasthan, Gujarat, and Tamil Nadu are at the forefront of solar energy generation, contributing significantly to the country's utility-scale solar capacity. Rajasthan, in particular, has surpassed its target of 30 GW capacity for 2024-25.
* Overall Renewable Energy Growth: India's total installed renewable energy (RE) capacity has reached 226.75 GW as of May 31, 2025, with solar power being the dominant source.

Key Solar Energy Programs and Initiatives:

* PM Surya Ghar: Muft Bijli Yojana (Launched Feb 2024):
* Aim: To provide free electricity to households by subsidizing the installation of rooftop solar panels.
* Target: To light up 1 crore (10 million) households and achieve 27 GW of rooftop solar capacity by March 2027.
* Progress: As of March 2025, the scheme had already achieved a milestone of 10 lakh (1 million) solar -powered homes. It has received 47.3 lakh applications and disbursed ₹4,770 crore in subsidi es to 6.13 lakh beneficiaries.
* Benefits: Free electricity (up to 300 units/month), reduced electricity bills, increased renewable energy adoption, reduced carbon emissions, and promotion of domestic manufacturing of solar modules and cells.
* "Model Solar Village" component: Aims to establish one Model Solar Village per district, promoting self-reliance in energy.

Jawaharlal Nehru National Solar Mission (JNNSM) (Launched 2010):

* Vision: To establish India as a global leader in solar energy and promote ecologically sustainable growth while addressing energy security challenges.
* Evolution: Initially set a target of 20 GW by 2022, which was later revised to 100 GW by 2022 (40 GW from rooftop solar and 60 GW from large-scale grid-connected projects). While the 100 GW target by 2022 was not fully met, the mission laid the groundwork for the massive growth seen today.
* Impact: Significantly expanded solar capacity, improved solar manufacturing, encouraged new technologies, and facilitated the deployment of off-grid solar applications (pumps, lighting, mini-grids) in rural areas. It also led to the establishment of large-scale solar parks like the Rewa Ultra Mega Solar Park.

Solar Park Scheme:

* Purpose: To facilitate the rapid development of large-scale solar power projects (typically 500 MW and above) by providing ready infrastructure like land and transmission facilities. This reduces risks and speeds up project implementation.

Viability Gap Funding (VGF) Scheme:

* Role: Provides financial support to make solar power projects more viable and attractive to investors, bridging the gap between the cost of generation and the achievable tariff.

PM-KUSUM Scheme:

* Focus: Decentralized solar power generation for agricultural use, promoting the installation of standalone solar pumps and solarization of existing grid-connected agricultural pumps. This reduces diesel consumption and grid strain.

International Solar Alliance (ISA):

* India's Leadership: India is a founder member and hosts the headquarters of the ISA, a global intergovernmental organization that works to promote solar energy adoption across its member countries. This showcases India's commitment to global solar energy development.

Challenges and Future Outlook:

Despite impressive progress, India's solar energy program faces challenges such as:

* Land Acquisition: Finding large tracts of land for utility-scale solar projects can be challenging.
* Grid Integration: Integrating increasing amounts of intermittent solar power into the grid requires advanced grid management, energy storage solutions, and flexible generation sources.
* Financing: While subsidies exist, securing long-term and affordable financing for all projects remains crucial.
* Manufacturing Capacity: While "Aatmanirbhar Bharat" (self-reliant India) promotes domestic manufacturing, reducing reliance on imports for solar components is an ongoing effort.

Overall View:

India's solar energy program is a cornerstone of its energy transition, driven by strong government policies, ambitious targets, and increasing private sector participation. The focus on both large-scale utility projects and decentralized rooftop solar, coupled with international collaborations and domestic manufacturing push, positions India as a global leader in solar energy. The ongoing initiatives demonstrate a clear commitment to leveraging solar power for energy security, economic growth, and climate action.

SOLAR ENEGY PROGRAMME IN INDIA AND DENMARK

India and Denmark have a strong and growing partnership in the energy sector, particularly focusing on renewable energy, including solar power. This collaboration is primarily driven by their "Green Strategic Partnership."

Here's a breakdown of their solar energy program and broader energy cooperation:

Key Aspects of India-Denmark Solar Energy Cooperation:

* Renewed Memorandum of Understanding (MoU): India and Denmark recently (May 2025) renewed their energy cooperation MoU, which was originally signed in June 2020. This renewal ensures continuity and expands the scope of their collaboration.
* Focus on Clean and Sustainable Energy Solutions: The renewed MoU emphasizes knowledge exchange and technological collaboration, particularly in clean and sustainable energy solutions, which includes solar power.
* Supporting India's Net-Zero Target: The partnership actively supports India's ambitious target of achieving net-zero emissions by 2070. Solar energy plays a crucial role in this goal.
* Advanced Areas of Collaboration: The renewed agreement broadens the partnership to cover advanced areas relevant to solar energy integration, such as:
* Power system modeling
* Integration of variable renewable energy (like solar and wind)
* Cross-border electricity trading
* Development of EV charging infrastructure (which can be powered by renewables)
* Knowledge Exchange and Training: Both countries emphasize increased knowledge exchange through expert interactions, joint training sessions, and study tours. This allows India to benefit from Denmark's extensive experience in integrating high shares of renewable energy into its grid.

* **India-Denmark Energy Partnership (INDEP)**:

This serves as the centrepiece for government-to-government cooperation on energy. While initially a 5-year program (2020-2024), it is likely to be extended. INDEP involves the Danish Ministry of Foreign Affairs, the Indian Ministry of New and Renewable Energy (MNRE), and the Indian Ministry of Power (MoP).

* Green Transition Alliance India (GTAI): This new alliance, led by the Embassy and Consulate General of Denmark in India, aims to foster sustainable energy growth in India by promoting collaboration between businesses, government bodies, research institutions, and financial entities. It has working groups focusing on Renewable Energy, Green Fuels, and Energy Efficiency.

India's Solar Energy Initiatives:

India has several significant domestic programs and initiatives to boost solar energy adoption:

* PM Surya Ghar: Muft Bijli Yojana: Launched in February 2024, this scheme is the world's largest domestic rooftop solar initiative. It aims to provide free electricity to households through subsidized rooftop solar panels and targets 27 GW of rooftop solar capacity by March 2027.
* Jawaharlal Nehru National Solar Mission (NSM): Launched in 2010, the NSM is a major initiative to promote ecologically sustainable growth and address India's energy security challenges by establishing India as a global leader in solar energy.
* Solar Park Scheme: This scheme facilitates the establishment of large-scale solar parks (generally 500 MW and above) by providing necessary infrastructure like land and transmission facilities.
* Rooftop Solar Scheme: This scheme encourages the installation of solar panels on rooftops.
* Viability Gap Funding (VGF) Scheme: This provides financial support to solar power projects.
* PM-KUSUM Scheme: This scheme focuses on installing off-grid solar pumps in rural areas and reducing dependence on the grid.
* International Solar Alliance (ISA): Proposed by India as a founder member and headquartered in India, the ISA is a global initiative to promote solar energy.

Denmark's Contribution:

Denmark is a global leader in renewable energy with ambitious climate targets. It brings valuable expertise in:

* Integrating High Shares of Renewable Energy: Denmark has decades of experience in integrating large shares of renewable energy into its grid while maintaining a world-class security of electricity supply.
* Offshore Wind: While not solely solar, Denmark's expertise in offshore wind contributes to the broader renewable energy landscape and grid stability.
* Power Sector Analysis and Energy Modeling: Danish expertise in these areas can help India optimize its power system for higher renewable energy penetration.
* Energy Planning and Market Design: Denmark can share its learnings on efficient power markets and energy planning.

In essence, the India-Denmark partnership in solar energy is a strategic collaboration that combines India's significant renewable energy ambitions and market scale with Denmark's technological expertise and experience in green energy transitions.

SOLAR ENERGY PROGRAMME IN INDIA AND CHINA

India and China stand out as the two biggest players in the global solar energy landscape, but their approaches, strengths, and roles differ significantly. While both are committed to massive solar expansion to meet energy demands and climate goals, China leads in sheer scale and manufacturing dominance, while India is rapidly catching up in deployment and focusing on building domestic capabilities.

COMPARISIOM

1. Scale of Deployment and Targets

China:

* Current Leader: China is by far the world's largest solar power producer and installer. Its installed solar capacity dwarfs that of any other nation.
* Rapid Growth: China consistently adds record amounts of solar capacity annually. In 2024, China added nearly 374 GW of renewable power, with three-quarters coming from solar.
* Ambitious Goals: China aims to have 1,200 GW of combined wind and solar capacity by 2030.
* Mega-Projects: China is known for developing enormous solar projects, including vast solar farms in deserts (e.g., the "Great Solar Wall" in Inner Mongolia planning around 100 GW by 2030) and a significant push for distributed solar (e.g., "whole county solar" model for residential rooftops).

India:

* Fast-Growing Market: India has one of the fastest-growing solar markets globally.
* Current Capacity: As of May 2025, India's total solar power installed capacity is approximately 110.83 GW.
* Ambitious 2030 Target: India has pledged to achieve 500 GW of non-fossil fuel-based electricity capacity by 2030, with solar expected to contribute around 300 GW of this total.
* Decentralized Focus: Alongside utility-scale projects, India has a strong emphasis on decentralized solutions like rooftop solar and solar pumps for agriculture.

2. Manufacturing Dominance and Supply Chain

China:

* Global Manufacturing Hub: China dominates almost every segment of the solar PV supply chain, from polysilicon and wafers to cells and modules. It accounts for an overwhelming majority (e.g., 95% of wafer manufacturing, over 80% of cell and module production globally).
* Cost Advantage: Chinese manufacturers benefit from economies of scale, lower labour costs, and subsidized energy prices, leading to significantly lower production costs for solar components compared to other countries. This has allowed them to offer highly competitive prices globally.

* Innovation Leader: Chinese companies are also leading in patent filings and R&D for solar technologies.

India:

* Growing Domestic Manufacturing: India is actively trying to build its domestic solar manufacturing capacity to reduce reliance on imports, particularly from China.
* PLI Scheme: The Production Linked Incentive (PLI) Scheme is a key government initiative providing financial incentives to encourage giga-scale manufacturing of high-efficiency solar PV modules in India.
* Import Dependence: Despite efforts, India remains heavily reliant on imports, especially for solar cells and wafers, with China being the dominant supplier (historically over 70-90% of imports, though recent trends show a slight decrease in China's share of cell imports).
* Higher Domestic Costs: Indian-made solar cells and modules are currently more expensive than Chinese imports, even after accounting for customs duties, due to higher raw material costs, smaller production scales, and less integrated supply chains.
* "China Plus One" Strategy: India aims to position itself as an alternative manufacturing hub for countries looking to diversify their supply chains away from China.

3. Government Policies and Support

China:

* Aggressive Industrial Policies: The Chinese government has provided massive subsidies, preferential loans, land, and R&D funding to its solar manufacturers, enabling them to scale rapidly and achieve global dominance.
* Centralized Planning: Strong top-down planning and execution of large-scale projects.
* Feed-in Tariffs (historically): China initially used generous feed-in tariffs to spur deployment, though these have been adjusted over time.

India:

* Supportive Policy Framework: India has implemented a robust policy framework, including:
* JNNSM (Jawaharlal Nehru National Solar Mission): The foundational policy.
* PM Surya Ghar: Muft Bijli Yojana: A massive residential rooftop solar subsidy program.
* PM-KUSUM Scheme: Solarization of agriculture.
* Solar Parks Scheme: Facilitating large-scale project development.
* PLI Scheme: For manufacturing.
* Waiver of Inter-State Transmission System (ISTS) Charges: For renewable energy.
* 100% FDI: Allowed in renewable energy.

* Emphasis on Local Content: Policies like the Approved List of Models and Manufacturers (ALMM) promote the use of domestically manufactured modules in government-tendered projects.
* Competitive Auctions: India largely relies on reverse auctions to procure solar power, which has driven down tariffs significantly.

4. Domestic Consumption vs. Export Focus

China:

* Massive Domestic Demand: While China is a huge exporter, its domestic market is also enormous, absorbing a significant portion of its production.
* Export Powerhouse: China is the world's largest exporter of solar PV products, supplying components and modules to countries across the globe.

India:

* Strong Domestic Demand: India's growing energy needs mean that most of its solar deployment is for domestic consumption.
* Emerging Exporter: India is increasingly looking to become an exporter of PV modules, with some Indian manufacturers already exporting to markets like the US. However, this is still a small fraction compared to China's export volume.
* Overcapacity Concerns: The sheer scale of Chinese manufacturing has led to concerns about overcapacity and potential dumping of solar products on international markets, affecting manufacturers in other countries.
* Grid Integration: Integrating massive amounts of intermittent solar power into its vast grid can pose challenges. India:
* Dependence on Imports: Despite efforts, heavy reliance on Chinese imports for critical components (especially cells and wafers) remains a vulnerability and impacts the cost-competitiveness of domestic manufacturing.
* Land Acquisition: Securing large tracts of land for utility-scale solar projects can be challenging.
* Financing and Grid Infrastructure: While improving, ensuring adequate financing and robust grid infrastructure for rapid scale-up is crucial.
* Rooftop Solar Implementation of rooftop solar, despite policy support, faces challenges related to consumer awareness, financing, and regulatory hurdles at the state level.

In essence, China's solar program is characterized by its unprecedented scale, deep manufacturing integration, and global market dominance, achieved through aggressive industrial policies. India's solar program, while also ambitious in deployment, is marked by a strong push for domestic manufacturing self-reliance, diversified applications (including

agriculture and residential), and strategic policy support to achieve its ambitious energy transition goals.

The housing societies or residential complexes demand is a growing area, especially with increasing awareness of renewable energy and rising electricity costs.

Here's a breakdown of how solar energy programs typically work for societies and the benefits they offer, especially in a country like India where there are significant government initiatives:

Understanding Solar Energy Programs for Housing Societies

These programs generally involve installing solar photovoltaic (PV) systems on common area rooftops within a residential complex or gated community. The electricity generated can be used for:

* Common Area Consumption: Powering shared facilities like:
* Staircase lighting
* Elevators
* Water pumps
* Clubhouses and gyms
* Streetlights within the society
* EV charging stations (a growing trend)
* Individual Household Consumption (via Net Metering): In many regions, excess solar energy generated by the society's system can be fed back into the main electricity grid. Through a mechanism called net metering, the society receives credits for this exported electricity, which can then be adjusted against the individual electricity bills of residents, or for the society's common area bills.

Key Benefits for Housing Societies:

* Significant Cost Savings: This is often the primary driver. By generating their own electricity, societies can drastically reduce or even eliminate their common area electricity bills. With net metering, individual residents can also see a reduction in their personal bills
* Reduced Carbon Footprint: Switching to solar significantly lowers reliance on fossil fuels, contributing to a cleaner environment and helping the society meet sustainability goals
* Energy Independence and Reliability: Solar power reduces dependence on the traditional grid, offering some protection against power outages and fluctuating electricity prices ncreased Property Value: Homes within solar-powered societies often see an increase in property value due as buyers increasingly look for energy-efficient and sustainable features.
* Low Maintenance Costs: Solar panel systems are generally durable and require minimal maintenance, mostly occasional cleaning and periodic inspections .

* Government Incentives and Subsidies: Many governments, like India's, offer significant financial assistance to

encourage solar adoption in residential sectors, making the initial investment more affordable . How Housing Societies Implement Solar Programs (General Steps):

* Feasibility Study: An assessment of the society's total energy consumption, available rooftop space, structural integrity, and shading analysis is conducted to determine the optimal size and capacity of the solar system
* Member Consent: Crucially, the society's members must approve the project, often through a resolution passed in an Annual General Meeting (AGM) (Source 2.2).
* Vendor Selection: Choosing a reputable and approved solar installer is key for quality installation and after-sales service Application for Subsidies & Approvals: The society, often with the help of the vendor, applies for government subsidies (e.g., PM Surya Ghar Muft Bijli Yojana in India) and obtains necessary approvals from the local electricity distribution company (DISCOM) (
* Installation and Commissioning: The solar panels, inverters, and other components are installed. The system is then inspected and approved by the DISCOM, which issues a commissioning certificate
* Net Metering Application: If applicable, the society applies for net metering to allow for the export of excess electricity to the grid .
* Maintenance and Monitoring: Regular cleaning and monitoring ensure optimal performance of the solar plant

Government Schemes (Example: India's PM Surya Ghar Muft Bijli Yojana)

India has a significant program called "PM Surya Ghar Muft Bijli Yojana" (also known as the Rooftop Solar Scheme) which was launched to promote rooftop solar installations in residential households, including Group Housing Societies (GHS) and Resident Welfare Associations (RWA))

* Subsidy Structure for Societies: For common facilities, including EV charging, the scheme offers a subsidy of ₹18,000 per kW for systems up to 500 kW capacity (with certain per-house limits)). This can translate into substantial savings for large societies (e.g., up to ₹90 lakhs for a 500 kW system)
* Process: The application process is typically online through a national portal, followed by feasibility clearance, installation by an approved vendor, and direct subsidy disbursal to the society's bank account,

If you could provide more specific details about the "Society Limited" aspect you're curious about (e.g., is it a specific organization, a type of residential society, or a program with limited scope?), I can give you even more tailored information!

FUTURE OF SOLAR ENERGY

The future of solar energy programs is incredibly promising, driven by rapid technological advancements, decreasing costs, and increasing global commitment to renewable energy. Here's a breakdown of key aspects:

1. Technological Advancements:

* Improved Solar Panel Efficiency: Ongoing research is leading to significantly higher conversion efficiencies, meaning more electricity can be generated from smaller areas. This includes:
* Perovskite Solar Cells: These are a game-changer, offering high efficiency at lower production costs. They can even be layered on top of traditional silicon cells (tandem cells) to capture more of the solar spectrum.
* Bifacial Solar Panels: These panels capture sunlight from both the front and back, increasing overall energy production.
* Thin-Film Solar Cells: Lightweight and flexible, these can be applied to various surfaces, including bendable and even transparent materials for building integration.
* Quantum Dot Solar Cells: A newer technology with potential for high efficiency and flexibility.
* Advanced Energy Storage Solutions: The intermittency of solar power is being addressed with improved battery technologies (e.g., lithium-ion, solid-state, and flow batteries) that can store excess energy for use during the night or cloudy periods.
* AI and Machine Learning: AI is revolutionizing solar by:
* Optimizing energy production and consumption in real-time.
* Improving solar energy forecasting for better grid management and energy planning.
* Predicting and minimizing solar curtailment.
* Building-Integrated Photovoltaics (BIPV): Solar panels are being seamlessly integrated into building materials like roofs, walls, and windows, offering both energy generation and aesthetic benefits.
* Floating Solar Farms: Installing solar panels on water bodies conserves land space and can even lead to higher efficiency due to cooling effects.
* Solar Tracking Systems: These systems allow panels to follow the sun's path throughout the day, maximizing energy capture.
* Night-Time Solar Plants: While still in early stages, research is exploring technologies that can generate power during the night.

2. Decreasing Costs:

* The cost of solar technology has fallen dramatically over the past decade, making solar installations more affordable and competitive with traditional energy sources. This trend is expected to continue with economies of scale in manufacturing.

3. Policy and Investment Support:

* Governments worldwide are implementing policies, incentives (like tax credits and subsidies), and ambitious renewable energy targets to accelerate solar adoption. India, for example, is a global leader in solar energy and aims to have 500 GW of renewable energy capacity by 2030, with a significant portion from solar.
* Significant foreign and domestic investments are flowing into the solar sector, driving growth and innovation.

4. Expanding Applications and Adoption:

* Rooftop Solar: This decentralized solution is gaining immense popularity for residential, commercial, and industrial buildings.
* Community Solar Programs: These allow multiple households or businesses to benefit from shared solar installations, making solar accessible to those with limited space or resources.
* Solar-Powered Transportation: Solar-powered electric vehicles and charging stations are becoming more prevalent.
* Rural Electrification: Solar energy is a viable solution for providing electricity to remote and underserved areas.
* Smart Cities: Solar energy will play a crucial role in powering urban infrastructure, smart grids, and IoT-based energy management systems.
* Solar Fuels: Research is ongoing into artificial photosynthesis to create solar fuels for energy storage and other applications.

Challenges to Overcome:

* Intermittency: Managing the variability of solar output due to weather conditions. This is being addressed through improved forecasting and energy storage.
* Grid Integration: Ensuring seamless integration of large-scale solar into existing grids.
* Land Use: For large solar farms, land availability can be a concern, leading to innovations like floating solar and agrivoltaics (combining agriculture with solar).
* Supply Chain and Raw Materials: Ensuring sustainable and ethical sourcing of materials for solar panel manufacturing.

In conclusion, the future of solar energy programs is characterized by continuous innovation, increasing affordability, and widespread adoption across diverse applications. Solar is poised to become the leading source of electricity globally, playing a pivotal role in transitioning towards a clean, sustainable, and energy-independent future.

The future of solar energy programs is incredibly promising, driven by rapid technological advancements, decreasing costs, and increasing global commitment to renewable energy. Here's a breakdown of key aspects:

1. Technological Advancements:

* Improved Solar Panel Efficiency: Ongoing research is leading to significantly higher conversion efficiencies, meaning more electricity can be generated from smaller areas. This includes:
* Perovskite Solar Cells: These are a game-changer, offering high efficiency at lower production costs. They can even be layered on top of traditional silicon cells (tandem cells) to capture more of the solar spectrum.
* Bifacial Solar Panels: These panels capture sunlight from both the front and back, increasing overall energy production.
* Thin-Film Solar Cells: Lightweight and flexible, these can be applied to various surfaces, including bendable and even transparent materials for building integration.
* Quantum Dot Solar Cells: A newer technology with potential for high efficiency and flexibility.
* Advanced Energy Storage Solutions: The intermittency of solar power is being addressed with improved battery technologies (e.g., lithium-ion, solid-state, and flow batteries) that can store excess energy for use during the night or cloudy periods.
* AI and Machine Learning: AI is revolutionizing solar by:
* Optimizing energy production and consumption in real-time.
* Improving solar energy forecasting for better grid management and energy planning.
* Predicting and minimizing solar curtailment.
* Building-Integrated Photovoltaics (BIPV): Solar panels are being seamlessly integrated into building materials like roofs, walls, and windows, offering both energy generation and aesthetic benefits.
* Floating Solar Farms: Installing solar panels on water bodies conserves land space and can even lead to higher efficiency due to cooling effects.
* Solar Tracking Systems: These systems allow panels to follow the sun's path throughout the day, maximizing energy capture.
* Night-Time Solar Plants: While still in early stages, research is exploring technologies that can generate power during the night.

2. **Decreasing Costs:**

* The cost of solar technology has fallen dramatically over the past decade, making solar installations more affordable and competitive with traditional energy sources. This trend is expected to continue with economies of scale in manufacturing.

3. **Policy and Investment Suppor**t:

* Governments worldwide are implementing policies, incentives (like tax credits and subsidies), and ambitious renewable energy targets to accelerate solar adoption. India, for example, is a global leader in solar energy and aims to have 500 GW of renewable energy capacity by 2030, with a significant portion from solar.
* Significant foreign and domestic investments are flowing into the solar sector, driving growth and innovation.

4. **Expanding Applications and Adoption**:

* Rooftop Solar: This decentralized solution is gaining immense popularity for residential, commercial, and industrial buildings.
* Community Solar Programs: These allow multiple households or businesses to benefit from shared solar installations, making solar accessible to those with limited space or resources.
* Solar-Powered Transportation: Solar-powered electric vehicles and charging stations are becoming more prevalent.
* Rural Electrification: Solar energy is a viable solution for providing electricity to remote and underserved areas.
* Smart Cities: Solar energy will play a crucial role in powering urban infrastructure, smart grids, and IoT-based energy management systems.
* Solar Fuels: Research is ongoing into artificial photosynthesis to create solar fuels for energy storage and other applications.

Challenges to Overcome:

* Intermittency: Managing the variability of solar output due to weather conditions. This is being addressed through improved forecasting and energy storage.
* Grid Integration: Ensuring seamless integration of large-scale solar into existing grids.
* Land Use: For large solar farms, land availability can be a concern, leading to innovations like floating solar and agrivoltaics (combining agriculture with solar).
* Supply Chain and Raw Materials: Ensuring sustainable and ethical sourcing of materials for solar panel manufacturing.

In conclusion, the future of solar energy programs is characterized by continuous innovation, increasing affordability, and widespread adoption across diverse applications. Solar is poised to become the leading source of electricity globally, playing a pivotal role in transitioning towards a clean, sustainable, and energy-independent future.

USE OF ADVANCED TOOLS IN SOLAR ENERGY PLANNLNG

Remote sensing and satellite imaging play a crucial and increasingly vital role in solar energy planning, from initial resource assessment to ongoing monitoring and maintenance of solar installations. Here's a breakdown of their key applications and advantages:

1. Solar Resource Assessment:

* Irradiance Measurement: Satellites equipped with specialized sensors can measure the amount of solar radiation (irradiance) reaching the Earth's surface. This data, often processed through complex models (like HELIOSAT), accounts for factors like cloud cover, atmospheric conditions (aerosols, water vapor), and geographic positioning. This is crucial for identifying areas with high solar energy potential, especially in regions with sparse ground-based measurement stations
* Long-term Climate Trends: Satellite data can provide solar resource estimates spanning decades, enabling the analysis of long-term climatic trends, which is essential for accurate energy yield predictions and risk mitigation for solar projects

Site Selection and Feasibility Analysis:

* Identifying Optimal Locations: High-resolution satellite imagery, often combined with AI and machine learning algorithms, helps identify suitable sites for solar farms and rooftop installations. This involves analyzing various factors:
* Land Use and Topography: Satellite imagery helps assess land cover, terrain (slopes, rugged landscapes), and identify areas that might hinder construction or panel efficiency. It can also help avoid environmentally sensitive areas (wetlands, habitats) and ensure compliance with zoning laws (.
* Shading Analysis: Advanced analytics can detect shading issues from nearby trees, buildings, and terrain, both permanent and seasonal, and even hourly variations. This optimizes panel placement for maximum energy production
* Proximity to Infrastructure: Satellite data allows for the assessment of a site's proximity to existing power grid infrastructure (substations, transmission lines) and transportation networks (roads), which minimizes energy losses and connection costs Rooftop Potential: For urban areas, satellite imagery can accurately measure roof size, angles, and detect obstacles like chimneys, enabling precise assessments of rooftop solar potential (Source 4.2).
* Cost-Effectiveness and Efficiency: Satellite-based methods reduce the need for expensive and time-consuming manual field surveys, allowing developers to analyze multiple sites simultaneously and make faster, data-driven decisions

Monitoring and Maintenance:

* Performance Monitoring: High-resolution satellite imagery can be used to monitor existing solar installations, track changes over time, assess performance, and identify maintenance needs. This includes detecting issues like dust accumulation or panel damage that might not be obvious from the ground Automated Detection: Automated segmentation algorithms can identify and delineate individual solar panels within images, which is essential for solar panel inspection, maintenance, and performance monitoring at scale).
* Reduced Human Inspection: Remote sensing technologies can reduce the need for manual inspections, increasing efficiency and safety, especially in hard-to-reach or remote locations .

4. Urban Planning and Policy Making:

* Informing Urban Planning: Satellite imagery helps urban planners and authorities regulate and incentivize solar energy adoption in specific regions by providing data on the distribution and density of solar panels (Source 1.2).
* Supporting Policy Work: By tracking solar adoption across vast areas, satellite data supports critical policy work tied to sustainable development goals (Source 4.3).

In essence, remote sensing and satellite imaging provide a comprehensive, efficient, and cost-effective approach to solar energy planning, from the initial assessment of solar resources to the strategic selection of sites and ongoing management of solar assets. This technology is crucial for optimizing energy production, reducing financial risks, and accelerating the global transition to renewable energy.

COMPUTER MODELING FOR SOLAR ENERGY PLANNING

Computer modeling plays an absolutely vital role in every stage of a solar energy program, from initial feasibility studies and design to operational optimization and long-term planning. It allows for the virtual testing of scenarios, prediction of performance, and identification of potential issues before any physical infrastructure is built, saving significant time, money, and resources.

Here's a detailed breakdown of the role of computer modeling in solar energy programs:

1. Feasibility Studies and Site Assessment:

* Solar Resource Assessment: Models use historical weather data (irradiance, temperature, wind speed) and satellite imagery to accurately estimate the available solar resource at a given location. This helps identify the most suitable sites for solar projects.
* Shading Analysis: Advanced 3D modeling can simulate shading from buildings, trees, and other obstructions throughout the day and year. This is crucial for optimizing panel placement to maximize energy capture and avoid "hot spots" caused by uneven illumination.

* Geospatial Analysis: Geographic Information Systems (GIS) are integrated with solar modeling to identify optimal land use, assess grid proximity, and evaluate environmental impacts for large-scale solar farms.

2. System Design and Sizing:

* Module and Inverter Sizing: Software helps determine the optimal number, type, and configuration of solar panels and inverters based on energy demand, available space, and budget.
* Performance Prediction (Energy Yield): This is perhaps the most critical application. Models simulate the energy output of a proposed solar system under various real-world conditions (temperature, irradiance, panel degradation, wiring losses, dust accumulation, etc.). This provides crucial data for financial projections and ensures the system meets energy targets.
* Layout Optimization: Computer-aided design (CAD) tools and specialized solar design software (like Aurora Solar, PVsyst, HelioScope, OpenSolar) allow engineers to design panel layouts that maximize energy density, minimize cable runs, and account for specific site constraints.
* Balance of System (BOS) Component Sizing: Modeling helps in sizing batteries for energy storage, charge controllers, wiring, and other components to ensure system stability and efficiency.
* System Reliability and Redundancy: Simulations can assess the impact of component failures and help design systems with appropriate redundancy to ensure continuous power supply.

3. Financial and Economic Analysis:

* Levelized Cost of Energy (LCOE) Calculation: Models help calculate the LCOE, which is a crucial metric for comparing the cost-effectiveness of solar energy with other sources.
* Return on Investment (ROI) and Payback Period: By integrating energy yield predictions with system costs and financial incentives (tax credits, subsidies, net metering), models can project the financial viability and payback period of a solar investment.
* Scenario Analysis: Engineers can run various "what-if" scenarios (e.g., changes in electricity prices, interest rates, government policies) to assess the financial risk and sensitivity of a project.

4. Operations and Maintenance (O&M):

* Performance Monitoring and Diagnostics: Computer models are used to establish baseline performance expectations. Real-time data from operational solar plants can then be compared against these models to detect under-performance, identify faults (e.g., shading, soiling, inverter issues), and optimize maintenance schedules.
* Predictive Maintenance: AI and machine learning models, trained on historical performance and weather data, can predict potential equipment failures before they occur, enabling proactive maintenance and minimizing downtime.

* Forecasting Solar Power Generation: Accurate short-term and long-term forecasts of solar power output are essential for grid operators to manage intermittency, balance supply and demand, and optimize grid stability. Computer models using meteorological data are key to this.

Research and Development (R&D):

* Material Science and Cell Design: Advanced simulations are used to model the behavior of new photovoltaic materials, optimize solar cell structures, and predict their efficiency and durability under various conditions.
* New Technology Assessment: Before physically prototyping, new solar technologies (e.g., perovskites, bifacial modules, concentrators) can be modeled to assess their theoretical performance and potential for commercialization.
* System Integration Studies: Models help understand how solar energy interacts with other energy sources (wind, hydro, conventional power plants) and energy storage systems within a larger grid, facilitating the design of smart grids.

Benefits of Computer Modeling:

* Cost Reduction: Minimizes expensive on-site testing and physical prototypes.
* Risk Mitigation: Identifies and addresses potential problems early in the design phase.
* Optimized Performance: Ensures the system is designed for maximum energy output and efficiency.
* Faster Development: Speeds up the design, planning, and deployment process.
* Enhanced Accuracy: Provides more reliable predictions than manual calculations.
* Informed Decision-Making: Equips stakeholders with comprehensive data for investment and operational decisions.

In essence, computer modeling is the backbone of modern solar energy programs, enabling precision, efficiency, and informed strategic choices that are crucial for the continued growth and success of solar power globally.

BENEFIT TO SOCIETY AND ENVIRNMENT

Solar energy programs, whether driven by government initiatives, private sector development, or community efforts, offer a wide array of benefits that positively impact individuals, economies, and the environment. Here's a comprehensive look at these advantages:

I. Economic Benefits:

* Reduced Electricity Bills: This is often the most immediate and tangible benefit for individuals and businesses. By generating their own electricity, consumers significantly lower or even eliminate their monthly utility bills.
* Long-Term Savings: Solar power systems have a long lifespan (25-30+ years), providing decades of free electricity after the initial investment, offering protection against rising electricity prices.
* Increased Property Value: Homes and commercial properties with solar installations often see an increase in their market value, as buyers are willing to pay a premium for reduced energy costs and environmental benefits.
* Job Creation: The solar industry is a significant job creator, spanning manufacturing, research and development, sales, installation, maintenance, and project development. This provides employment opportunities across various skill levels.
* Economic Development: Large-scale solar projects attract investment, stimulate local economies, and can diversify revenue streams for communities through property taxes, sales taxes, and permitting fees.
* Energy Independence and Security: By reducing reliance on imported fossil fuels, countries and regions enhance their energy security and become less vulnerable to global energy price fluctuations and geopolitical instability.
* Return on Investment (ROI): With decreasing solar technology costs and various incentives, solar installations often offer a competitive return on investment, making them financially attractive.
* Incentives and Subsidies: Many governments offer significant financial incentives like tax credits, rebates, feed-in tariffs, and low-interest loans to encourage solar adoption, making it more accessible and affordable. For example, India's "PM Surya Ghar: Muft Bijli Yojana" aims to provide free electricity to households through subsidized rooftop solar panels.
* Income Generation (Net Metering): In many areas, solar owners can sell excess electricity generated by their systems back to the grid, creating an additional income stream.

II. Environmental Benefits:

* Reduced Greenhouse Gas Emissions: Solar energy produces no greenhouse gas emissions during operation, directly combating climate change by reducing the carbon t **Benefits associated with electricity generation.**
* Cleaner Air: By displacing fossil fuel combustion, solar power significantly reduces the release of harmful air pollutants like sulphur dioxide, nitrogen oxides, and particulate matter, leading to cleaner air and improved public health.

* Water Conservation: Unlike traditional thermal power plants that require vast amounts of water for cooling, solar PV systems use minimal water during operation,conserving this precious resource.
* Reduced Land Degradation: While large solar farms require land, rooftop solar installations utilize existing unused space, minimizing the need for new land clearing. Advancements like agrivoltaics (combining solar with agriculture) also promote sustainable land use.
* Conservation of Natural Resources: Solar power reduces the need for extraction and transportation of finite fossil fuels, preserving natural resources and minimizing the environmental impact of mining and drilling.

Social Benefits:

* Improved Public Health: Cleaner air translates to fewer respiratory illnesses, heart conditions, and other health issues, leading to healthier communities.
* Enhanced Energy Access and Equity: Solar energy, particularly through decentralized solutions like rooftop solar and mini-grids, brings electricity to remote and underserved communities that may not have access to the main grid. This can bridge energy inequality gaps.
* Better Education: Reliable electricity enables lighting for schools, allowing students to study after dark and providing power for computers and other educational technologies, especially in rural areas.
* Improved Healthcare: Solar power provides reliable electricity for clinics and hospitals, enabling refrigeration for vaccines and medicines, powering medical equipment, and ensuring lights for critical services.
* Empowerment of Communities: Decentralized solar gives communities more control over their energy supply, fostering self-sufficiency and resilience, especially important during power outages or natural disasters.
* Increased Safety and Security: Street lighting powered by solar enhances safety in public spaces and homes after dark.
* Sustainable Development: Solar energy aligns perfectly with sustainable development goals, promoting a balanced approach to economic growth, social equity, and environmental protection.
* Technological Advancement: Investments in solar energy spur innovation and research in related fields, leading to new technologies and solutions.

In conclusion, solar energy programs offer a powerful combination of economic, environmental, and social benefits, making them a crucial component of a sustainable and prosperous future for mankind.

Solar energy programs, whether driven by government initiatives, private sector development, or community efforts, offer a wide array of benefits that positively impact individuals, economies, and the environment.

[Economic Benefits:

* Reduced Electricity Bills: This is often the most immediate and tangible benefit for individuals and businesses. By generating their own electricity, consumers significantly lower or even eliminate their monthly utility bills.
* Long-Term Savings: Solar power systems have a long lifespan (25-30+ years), providing decades of free electricity after the initial investment, offering protection against rising electricity prices.
* Increased Property Value: Homes and commercial properties with solar installations often see an increase in their market value, as buyers are willing to pay a premium for reduced energy costs and environmental benefits.
* Job Creation: The solar industry is a significant job creator, spanning manufacturing, research and development, sales, installation, maintenance, and project development. This provides employment opportunities across various skill levels.
* Economic Development: Large-scale solar projects attract investment, stimulate local economies, and can diversify revenue streams for communities through property taxes, sales taxes, and permitting fees.
* Energy Independence and Security: By reducing reliance on imported fossil fuels, countries and regions enhance their energy security and become less vulnerable to global energy price fluctuations and geopolitical instability.
* Return on Investment (ROI): With decreasing solar technology costs and various incentives, solar installations often offer a competitive return on investment, making them financially attractive.
* Incentives and Subsidies: Many governments offer significant financial incentives like tax credits, rebates, feed-in tariffs, and low-interest loans to encourage solar adoption, making it more accessible and affordable. For example, India's "PM Surya Ghar: Muft Bijli Yojana" aims to provide free electricity to households through subsidized rooftop solar panels.
* Income Generation (Net Metering): In many areas, solar owners can sell excess electricity generated by their systems back to the grid, creating an additional income stream.

I. Environmental Benefits:

* Reduced Greenhouse Gas Emissions: Solar energy produces no greenhouse gas emissions during operation, directly combating climate change by reducing the carbon footprint associated with electricity generation.

* Cleaner Air: By displacing fossil fuel combustion, solar power significantly reduces the release of harmful air pollutants like sulfur dioxide, nitrogen oxides, and particulate matter, leading to cleaner air and improved public health.
* Water Conservation: Unlike traditional thermal power plants that require vast amounts of water for cooling, solar PV systems use minimal water during operation, conserving this precious resource.
* Reduced Land Degradation: While large solar farms require land, rooftop solar installations utilize existing unused space, minimizing the need for new land clearing. Advancements like agrivoltaics (combining solar with agriculture) also promote sustainable land use.
* Conservation of Natural Resources: Solar power reduces the need for extraction and transportation of finite fossil fuels, preserving natural resources and minimizing the environmental impact of mining and drilling.

II. Social Benefits:

* Improved Public Health: Cleaner air translates to fewer respiratory illnesses, heart conditions, and other health issues, leading to healthier communities.
* Enhanced Energy Access and Equity: Solar energy, particularly through decentralized solutions like rooftop solar and mini-grids, brings electricity to remote and underserved communities that may not have access to the main grid. This can bridge energy inequality gaps.
* Better Education: Reliable electricity enables lighting for schools, allowing students to study after dark and providing power for computers and other educational technologies, especially in rural areas.
* Improved Healthcare: Solar power provides reliable electricity for clinics and hospitals, enabling refrigeration for vaccines and medicines, powering medical equipment, and ensuring lights for critical services.
* Empowerment of Communities: Decentralized solar gives communities more control over their energy supply, fostering self-sufficiency and resilience, especially important during power outages or natural disast Increased Safety and Security: Street lighting powered by solar enhances safety in public spaces and homes after dark.
* Sustainable Development: Solar energy aligns perfectly with sustainable development goals, promoting a balanced approach to economic growth, social equity, and environmental protection.
* Technological Advancement: Investments in solar energy spur innovation and research in related fields, leading to new technologies and solutions.

In conclusion, solar energy programs offer a powerful combination of economic, environmental, and social benefits, making them a crucial component of a sustainable and prosperous future for mankind.

CONCLUSION

Solar energy plays a transformative and multifaceted role in the upliftment of mankind, impacting various aspects of human well-being, economic development, and environmental sustainability.

1. Poverty Alleviation and Economic Empowerment:

* Access to Affordable Energy: For billions globally, particularly in developing nations and rural areas, reliable electricity is a luxury. Solar power offers a decentralized, cost-effective solution, bypassing expensive grid infrastructure. This means homes can have lighting, allowing children to study after dark and improving safety.
* Reduced Energy Costs: By generating their own electricity, individuals and businesses can significantly reduce or even eliminate their reliance on expensive, often polluting, fossil fuels (like kerosene or diesel generators). This frees up household income for other necessities and makes businesses more competitive.
* Job Creation: The solar industry is a booming sector, creating jobs in manufacturing, installation, maintenance, and research. This provides stable and often higher-paying employment opportunities, particularly in regions where they are desperately needed.
* Local Economic Development: Solar mini-grids and off-grid solutions empower local communities to establish small businesses (e.g., charging stations, small shops with refrigeration, artisan workshops) that can thrive with reliable power, leading to local economic growth and reduced migration to urban centers.
* Increased Productivity: Businesses can operate longer hours, use modern machinery, and improve efficiency with consistent power, leading to increased output and income.

Improved Health and Well-being:

* Clean Air and Reduced Respiratory Illnesses: By replacing fossil fuels, solar energy dramatically reduces air pollution, including particulate matter, sulfur dioxide, and nitrogen oxides. This leads to fewer respiratory illnesses, heart disease, and other health problems, particularly benefiting vulnerable populations like children and the elderly.
* Refrigeration for Vaccines and Medicines: In areas without reliable electricity, clinics and hospitals often struggle to store temperature-sensitive vaccines and medicines. Solar-powered refrigeration ensures these vital supplies remain effective, directly impacting public health and reducing preventable diseases.
* Enhanced Healthcare Services: Solar power enables 24/7 operation of lights, medical equipment, and communication systems in health facilities, improving diagnostic capabilities, surgical conditions, and overall patient care, especially during emergencies.

* Access to Clean Water: Solar-powered pumps can provide access to clean, potable water for drinking and sanitation, significantly reducing waterborne diseases and improving hygiene.

2. Enhanced Education:

* Lighting for Schools: Solar lights extend learning hours in schools, allowing students to study in the evenings. It also enables the use of computers and other educational technologies.
* Digital Inclusion: Solar power facilitates the use of computers, internet access, and other digital learning tools, bridging the digital divide and providing access to a wealth of educational resources.
* Improved Safety and Security: Well-lit schools and homes contribute to a safer environment for students and communities.

Climate Change Mitigation and Environmental Protection:

* Reduced Greenhouse Gas Emissions: Solar energy is a clean, renewable source that produces no greenhouse gas emissions during operation. This is crucial in combating climate change, reducing global warming, and mitigating its devastating effects like extreme weather events and rising sea levels.
* Conservation of Natural Resources: By reducing reliance on fossil fuels, solar energy helps conserve finite resources and minimizes the environmental damage associated with their extraction and combustion.
* Reduced Water Consumption: Unlike many traditional power plants, solar power generation requires minimal water, a critical benefit in water-stressed regions.
* Protection of Biodiversity: By reducing the need for destructive energy practices, solar energy contributes to the preservation of ecosystems and biodiversity.

3. Energy Security and Independence:

* Decentralized Power: Solar panels can be installed locally, reducing reliance on centralized grids and long- distance transmission lines, which are vulnerable to outages and natural disasters. This enhances energy resilience for communities.
* Reduced Geopolitical Dependence: Countries can lessen their reliance on imported fossil fuels, leading to greater energy independence and national security.
* Empowerment of Communities: Communities become more self-sufficient in their energy needs, fostering a sense of ownership and control over their future.

In essence, solar energy is not just about generating electricity; it's a powerful tool for sustainable development, empowering communities, improving livelihoods, and building a healthier, more equitable future for all of mankind.

India's solar energy program is a rapidly expanding and ambitious undertaking, aiming to transform the nation's energy landscape and meet its climate commitments. Here's an overview of its current status and key initiatives:

Current Status and Achievements (as of May 2025):

* Significant Installed Capacity: India's cumulative solar power capacity has reached 110.83 GW as of May 31, 2025. This includes:
* Ground Mounted Solar Plants: 84.43 GW
* Grid Connected Solar Rooftop: 18.37 GW
* Hybrid Projects (Solar Component): 3.02 GW
* Off-Grid Solar: 5.01 GW
* Rapid Growth: Solar energy continues to be the largest contributor to India's renewable energy capacity expansion. In the Financial Year 2024-25, India added a remarkable 23.83 GW of solar capacity.
* Leading States: Rajasthan, Gujarat, and Tamil Nadu are at the forefront of solar energy generation, contributing significantly to the country's utility-scale solar capacity. Rajasthan, in particular, has surpassed its target of 30 GW capacity for 2024-25.
* Overall Renewable Energy Growth: India's total installed renewable energy (RE) capacity has reached 226.75 GW as of May 31, 2025, with solar power being the dominant source.

Key Solar Energy Programs and Initiatives:

* PM Surya Ghar: Muft Bijli Yojana (Launched Feb 2024):
* Aim: To provide free electricity to households by subsidizing the installation of rooftop solar panels.
* Target: To light up 1 crore (10 million) households and achieve 27 GW of rooftop solar capacity by March 2027.
* Progress: As of March 2025, the scheme had already achieved a milestone of 10 lakh (1 million) solar-powered homes. It has received 47.3 lakh applications and disbursed ₹4,770 crore in subsidies to 6.13 lakh beneficiaries.
* Benefits: Free electricity (up to 300 units/month), reduced electricity bills, increased renewable energy adoption, reduced carbon emissions, and promotion of domestic manufacturing of solar modules and cells.
* "Model Solar Village" component: Aims to establish one Model Solar Village per district, promoting self-reliance in energy.
* Jawaharlal Nehru National Solar Mission (JNNSM) (Launched 2010):

* Vision: To establish India as a global leader in solar energy and promote ecologically sustainable growth while addressing energy security challenges.
* Evolution: Initially set a target of 20 GW by 2022, which was later revised to 100 GW by 2022 (40 GW from rooftop solar and 60 GW from large-scale grid-connected projects). While the 100 GW target by 2022 was not fully met, the mission laid the groundwork for the massive growth seen today.
* Impact: Significantly expanded solar capacity, improved solar manufacturing, encouraged new technologies, and facilitated the deployment of off-grid solar applications (pumps, lighting, mini-grids) in rural areas. It also led to the establishment of large-scale solar parks like the Rewa Ultra Mega Solar Park.

Solar Park Scheme:

* Purpose: To facilitate the rapid development of large-scale solar power projects (typically 500 MW and above) by providing ready infrastructure like land and transmission facilities. This reduces risks and speeds up project implementation.

Viability Gap Funding (VGF) Scheme:

* Role: Provides financial support to make solar power projects more viable and attractive to investors, bridging the gap between the cost of generation and the achievable tariff.

PM-KUSUM Scheme:

* Focus: Decentralized solar power generation for agricultural use, promoting the installation of standalone solar pumps and solarization of existing grid-connected agricultural pumps. This reduces diesel consumption and grid strain.

International Solar Alliance (ISA):

* India's Leadership: India is a founder member and hosts the headquarters of the ISA, a global intergovernmental organization that works to promote solar energy adoption across its member countries. This showcases India's commitment to global solar energy development.

Challenges and Future Outlook:

* Land Acquisition: Finding large tracts of land for utility-scale solar projects can be challenging.
* Grid Integration: Integrating increasing amounts of intermittent solar power into the grid requires advanced grid management, energy storage solutions, and flexible generation sources.
* Financing: While subsidies exist, securing long-term and affordable financing for all projects remains crucial.

* Manufacturing Capacity: While "Aatmanirbhar Bharat" (self-reliant India) promotes domestic manufacturing, reducing reliance on imports for solar components is an ongoing effort.

vising the maintenance team on necessary repairs or further inspections, enabling timely scheduling.

* Documentation & Trending: Keeping records to track machine health over time and support continuous improvement.

Typical Equipment Monitored:

* Electric Motors
* Pumps
* Fans & Blowers
* Gearboxes
* Compressors
* Turbines
* Machine Tools

In summary, a vibration program shifts maintenance from a reactive "fix-it-when-it-breaks" approach to a proactive "predict-and-prevent" strategy, significantly enhancing operational reliability and cost-efficiency in industrial settings.

Do you have any specific aspect of a vibration program you'd like to know more about? For instance, specific types of faults, analysis techniques, or the required equipment?

SECI" stands for Solar Energy Corporation of India Limited. It is a crucial entity in India's renewable energy landscape, and its role has been expanding significantly.

You will see SECI playing a pivotal role in India's solar (and broader renewable) energy program because it acts as the primary implementing agency for many of the government's initiatives and schemes.

Here's a breakdown of "why you will see SECI":

* Facilitating India's Ambitious Renewable Energy Targets:
* India has pledged to achieve 500 GW of non-fossil fuel-based energy capacity by 2030. SECI is the nodal agency designated to help meet these ambitious targets, with solar contributing a significant portion.
* It plays a central role in India's Nationally Determined Contributions (NDCs) under the Paris Agreement.
* Competitive Bidding and Project Development:

* SECI is the main entity that conducts competitive, tariff-based e-bidding for large-scale solar, wind, hybrid, and now even Round-The-Clock (RTC) and Firm and Dispatchable Renewable Energy (FDRE) projects across India.
* It floats tenders, evaluates bids, and selects renewable energy (RE) developers. As of May 1, 2025, SECI has awarded over 73.8 GW of renewable energy capacity through this process.
* Power Procurement and Trading (Intermediary Role):
* SECI acts as a power procurement intermediary. It signs long-term (e.g., 25-year) Power Purchase Agreements (PPAs) with project developers to buy electricity.
* It then signs back-to-back Power Sale Agreements (PSAs) with state electricity distribution companies (DISCOMs) or other off-takers to sell this renewable power.
* This unique model provides payment security to developers (as SECI generally has a higher credit rating than many DISCOMs), making projects more bankable and attractive to investors. This has been instrumental in driving down solar tariffs in India to record lows.
* Implementation of Government Schemes:
* SECI is the key implementing agency for various schemes under the Ministry of New and Renewable Energy (MNRE), such as:
* Solar Park Scheme: Developing large-scale solar parks with shared infrastructure.
* Grid-Connected Rooftop Solar Programme: Promoting rooftop solar installations.
* Various schemes involving Central Financial Assistance (CFA) disbursement.
* Pioneering New Technologies and Business Areas:
* SECI is not just focused on traditional solar and wind. It's actively venturing into and driving emerging areas crucial for India's energy transition:
* Green Hydrogen and Green Ammonia: SECI is launching tenders for the offtake of green ammonia to decarbonize industries like fertilizer production, aligning with India's National Green Hydrogen Mission.
* Energy Storage Systems: Developing utility-scale battery energy storage projects to address grid intermittency.
* Greening the Transport Sector: Exploring solutions for electric vehicle charging infrastructure with renewable energy.
* Offshore Wind Energy: Involved in the leasing and development of offshore wind projects.
* Waste-to-Energy.
* Own Project Development and Consultancy:
* Beyond its role as a facilitator, SECI also sets up and owns renewable energy projects directly.
* It offers Project Management Consultancy (PMC) services to other public sector and government entities for their RE projects, providing expertise from feasibility studies to commissioning.
* Credibility and Trust:

* As a "Navratna" Central Public Sector Undertaking (CPSU), SECI holds a high level of credibility. Its transparent e-bidding process and robust payment security mechanism have fostered trust among developers and investors, leading to high participation rates in its tenders.

In summary, SECI it is the central engine and key orchestrator behind India's massive renewable energy deployment, particularly in solar. Its unique business model, role in policy implementation, and expansion into new green technologies make it indispensable for India's journey towards a sustainable and energy-secure future.

V IABILITY OF SOLAR ENERGY PROGRAMME

The viability of solar energy in India is exceptionally strong and continues to grow. It is not just viable, but a critical and indispensable component of India's energy future.

Here's a breakdown of the factors contributing to its viability:

Strong Fundamentals for Viability

* **Abundant Solar Resourc**e:
* India is a tropical country blessed with high solar insolation. Most parts of the country receive 4-7 kWh per square meter per day of solar energy, with an average of 300 clear and sunny days in a year.
* The total assessed solar power potential is a massive 10,830 GW, far exceeding India's current or projected energy demand.

Decreasing Costs of Solar Technology:

* The cost of solar panels (PV modules) has dropped dramatically over the past decade, making solar power highly competitive, even without subsidies, with traditional fossil fuel sources. India has seen some of the lowest solar tariffs globally through competitive bidding.
* Technological advancements continue to improve panel efficiency and reduce installation costs.
* Ambitious Government Policies and Targets:
* India has committed to achieving 500 GW of non-fossil fuel-based energy capacity by 2030, with solar expected to contribute around 300 GW of this.
* Key schemes like PM Surya Ghar: Muft Bijli Yojana (for residential rooftop solar), PM-KUSUM (for agriculture), and Solar Park Scheme (for utility-scale projects) provide significant financial incentives and infrastructure support.
* Policies like Production Linked Incentive (PLI) scheme are boosting domestic manufacturing, enhancing long- term viability by reducing import dependence.

* Renewable Purchase Obligations (RPOs) mandate utilities to procure renewable power, ensuring a market for solar energy.
* High and Growing Energy Demand:
* India's rapidly growing economy and population necessitate a massive increase in energy supply. Solar energy provides a clean and sustainable way to meet this escalating demand.
* Environmental Imperative:
* Solar power helps India meet its climate change commitments (e.g., Net-Zero by 2070) by significantly reducing carbon emissions and air pollution from fossil fuels. This environmental benefit enhances its long-term societal viability.

Economic Benefits:

* Job Creation: The solar sector is a significant employer, creating jobs in manufacturing, installation, operations, and maintenance.
* Energy Security: Reduces reliance on volatile global fossil fuel markets, saving foreign exchange.
* Financial Savings for Consumers/Businesses: Rooftop solar systems, in particular, offer substantial savings on electricity bills, with payback periods often ranging from 4-7 years, making them economically attractive for individual consumers and industries.
* Attracting Investment: The robust policy framework and growth potential attract significant domestic and foreign investment.

Challenges Affecting Viability (and how they're being addressed) While viability is high, certain challenges need continuous attention:

* Grid Integration and Intermittency:

Challenge:

Solar's intermittent nature (only generates when the sun shines) poses grid balancing challenges, especially at high penetration levels.

* Addressing: Investment in energy storage solutions (batteries, pumped hydro), smart grid technologies, forecasting improvements, and hybrid projects (solar-wind hybrids) are underway. SECI is actively tendering for storage and firm & dispatchable renewable energy.

Land Acquisition:

* Challenge: Large utility-scale solar projects require vast tracts of land, which can be challenging to acquire in a densely populated country.

* Addressing: Development of solar parks streamlines land acquisition. Focus on rooftop solar and agri-PV (agrivoltaics) reduces reliance on new land. Utilization of "wastelands" is also a strategy.

Financing and DISCOM Health:

* Challenge: High upfront capital costs for large projects, and financial stress of some state electricity distribution companies (DISCOMs) can affect timely payments to developers.
* Addressing: Government schemes offer Viability Gap Funding (VGF). Agencies like SECI act as intermediaries to provide payment security. Reforms in the power sector and efforts to improve DISCOM finances are ongoing.

Domestic Manufacturing Scale and Competitiveness:

* Challenge: Despite growth, India still heavily relies on imports for solar cells and wafers, affecting the "Make in India" vision.
* Addressing: The PLI scheme is specifically designed to overcome this by incentivizing large-scale, integrated domestic manufacturing, aiming to build a self-reliant solar supply chain.
* Rooftop Solar Adoption:
* Challenge: Despite strong economic viability for consumers, rooftop solar has faced hurdles like lack of awareness, complex procedures, and initial financial outlay.
* Addressing: The new PM Surya Ghar: Muft Bijli Yojana aims to directly tackle these by providing substantial .

Conclusion

The viability of solar energy in India is undeniable and robust. The combination of abundant resources, drastically falling costs, strong government backing, and an urgent need for clean energy makes solar an extremely attractive and essential investment for India's future. While challenges exist, they are recognized and actively being addressed through comprehensive policies and strategic initiatives, ensuring that solar continues to be a driving force in India's energy transition.

India's solar energy program is a rapidly expanding and ambitious undertaking, aiming to transform the nation's energy landscape and meet its climate commitments. Here's an overview of its current status and key initiatives:

Current Status and Achievements (as of May 2025):

* Significant Installed Capacity: India's cumulative solar power capacity has reached 110.83 GW as of May 31, 2025. This includes:
* Ground Mounted Solar Plants: 84.43 GW

* Grid Connected Solar Rooftop: 18.37 GW
* Hybrid Projects (Solar Component): 3.02 GW
* Off-Grid Solar: 5.01 GW
* Rapid Growth: Solar energy continues to be the largest contributor to India's renewable energy capacity expansion. In the Financial Year 2024-25, India added a remarkable 23.83 GW of solar capacity.
* Leading States: Rajasthan, Gujarat, and Tamil Nadu are at the forefront of solar energy generation, contributing significantly to the country's utility-scale solar capacity. Rajasthan, in particular, has surpassed its target of 30 GW capacity for 2024-25.
* Overall Renewable Energy Growth: India's total installed renewable energy (RE) capacity has reached 226.75 GW as of May 31, 2025, with solar power being the dominant source.

Key Solar Energy Programs and Initiatives:

* PM Surya Ghar: Muft Bijli Yojana (Launched Feb 2024):
* Aim: To provide free electricity to households by subsidizing the installation of rooftop solar panels.
* Target: To light up 1 crore (10 million) households and achieve 27 GW of rooftop solar capacity by March 2027.
* Progress: As of March 2025, the scheme had already achieved a milestone of 10 lakh (1 million) solar-powered homes. It has received 47.3 lakh applications and disbursed ₹4,770 crore in subsidies to 6.13 lakh beneficiaries.
* Benefits: Free electricity (up to 300 units/month), reduced electricity bills, increased renewable energy adoption, reduced carbon emissions, and promotion of domestic manufacturing of solar modules and cells.
* "Model Solar Village" component: Aims to establish one Model Solar Village per district, promoting self-reliance in energy.
* Jawaharlal Nehru National Solar Mission (JNNSM) (Launched 2010):
* Vision: To establish India as a global leader in solar energy and promote ecologically sustainable growth while addressing energy security challenges.
* Evolution: Initially set a target of 20 GW by 2022, which was later revised to 100 GW by 2022 (40 GW from rooftop solar and 60 GW from large-scale grid-connected projects). While the 100 GW target by 2022 was not fully met, the mission laid the groundwork for the massive growth seen today.
* Impact: Significantly expanded solar capacity, improved solar manufacturing, encouraged new technologies, and facilitated the deployment of off-grid solar applications (pumps, lighting, mini-grids) in rural areas. It also led to the establishment of large-scale solar parks like the Rewa Ultra Mega Solar Park.

Solar Park Scheme:

* Purpose: To facilitate the rapid development of large-scale solar power projects (typically 500 MW and above) by providing ready infrastructure like land and transmission facilities. This reduces risks and speeds up project implementation.
* Viability Gap Funding (VGF) Scheme:
* Role: Provides financial support to make solar power projects more viable and attractive to investors, bridging the gap between the cost of generation and the achievable tariff.
* PM-KUSUM Scheme:
* Focus: Decentralized solar power generation for agricultural use, promoting the installation of standalone solar pumps and solarization of existing grid-connected agricultural pumps. This reduces diesel consumption and grid strain.
* International Solar Alliance (ISA):
* India's Leadership: India is a founder member and hosts the headquarters of the ISA, a global intergovernmental organization that works to promote solar energy adoption across its member countries. This showcases India's commitment to global solar energy development.

Challenges and Future Outlook:

Despite impressive progress, India's solar energy program faces challenges such as:

* Land Acquisition: Finding large tracts of land for utility-scale solar projects can be challenging.
* Grid Integration: Integrating increasing amounts of intermittent solar power into the grid requires advanced grid management, energy storage solutions, and flexible generation sources.
* Financing: While subsidies exist, securing long-term and affordable financing for all projects remains crucial.
* Manufacturing Capacity: While "Aatmanirbhar Bharat" (self-reliant India) promotes domestic manufacturing, reducing reliance on imports for solar components is an ongoing effort.

India's solar energy program is a cornerstone of its energy transition, driven by strong government policies, ambitious targets, and increasing private sector participation. The focus on both large-scale utility projects and decentralized rooftop solar, coupled with international collaborations and domestic manufacturing push, positions India as a global leader in solar energy. The ongoing initiatives demonstrate a clear commitment to leveraging solar power for energy security, economic growth, and climate action.

Sociological impact of solar energy programs.

* How do solar energy programs affect community development and social equity?
* What are the social benefits and drawbacks of transitioning to solar energy?
* What is the impact of solar energy adoption on local employment and economic structures?

* sociological impact of solar energy adoption
* community perceptions of solar energy projects
* social justice solar energy
* indigenous communities solar energy impact
* gender roles solar energy development
* solar energy and local governance

Senerzisisation the information gathered to provide a comprehensive answer on the sociological impact of solar energy programs, covering various aspects such as community development, social equity, employment, local perceptions, and potential challenges.

* How do solar energy programs affect community development and social equity?
* What are the social benefits and drawbacks of transitioning to solar energy?
* What is the impact of solar energy adoption on local employment and economic structures?
* sociological impact of solar energy adoption
* community perceptions of solar energy projects
* social justice solar energy
* indigenous communities solar energy impact
* gender roles solar energy development
* solar energy and local governance

Solar energy programs have far-reaching sociological impacts, influencing communities in diverse ways, from economic empowerment to shifts in social dynamics and perceptions.

Here's a breakdown of the key socal

1. Community Development and Energy Access:

* Bridging the Energy Divide: Solar energy is crucial for addressing energy poverty, especially in rural and remote areas where traditional grid infrastructure is lacking or unreliable. By providing access to clean and affordable electricity, solar programs can significantly enhance the quality of life, powering homes, schools, medical facilities, and small businesses after dark
* Improved Health and Education: Reliable electricity from solar can support better lighting for studying, refrigeration for medicines and food, and power for communication devices, leading to improved health outcomes and educational opportunities (Source 7.2). For instance, in indigenous communities, solar-powered water supply schemes have reduced the burden of water collection, particularly for women, and improved access to clean drinking water, leading to a decrease in waterborne illnesses
* Resilience and Disaster Preparedness: Solar systems, especially when paired with battery storage, offer energy independence and resilience during power outages caused by natural disasters or grid failures, allowing communities to recover faster .

Economic Empowerment and Livelihoods:

* Job Creation: The solar industry creates a wide range of jobs across its value chain, including manufacturing, installation, operations, maintenance, and project development. This can stimulate local economies and provide stable, profitable employment opportunities, particularly in construction and electrical engineering fields (Local Economic Benefits: Large-scale solar projects can significantly boost local tax revenues through property taxes, sales taxes, and permitting fees. This revenue can then be reinvested in public services, infrastructure (schools, roads, emergency services), and community development initiative
* Entrepreneurship and Small Businesses: Affordable and reliable solar power can enable small businesses to operate more efficiently and expand, fostering local economic growth and empowering communities (Source 1.2).
* Potential for Displacement: While generally positive, large-scale solar farms require significant land. In some cases, this can lead to concerns about land acquisition, potential displacement of agricultural workers or farmers, and changes in traditional livelihoods, especially if not managed with proper social safeguards and compensation (Source 6.2).

Social Equity and Justice (Energy Justice):

* Equitable Distribution of Benefits: The concept of "energy justice" is critical in solar energy transitions, aiming to ensure that the benefits of solar are fairly distributed among all members of society, particularly low-income and marginalized communities (Source 6.1).
* Community Solar Programs: These programs are designed to increase access to solar energy for those who cannot install panels on their own roofs (e.g., renters, apartment dwellers, low-income households), providing reduced energy costs and fostering community engagement
* Addressing Historical Inequities: Solar programs can be intentionally designed to address historical inequities by prioritizing investments in underserved communities, providing training and job opportunities, and ensuring fair participation in decision-making processes.

2. Community Perceptions and Acceptance:

* Generally Positive Attitudes: Studies indicate that residents living near large-scale solar energy developments often hold positive attitudes towards these projects, frequently outnumbering negative attitudes. Support tends to increase over time as communities experience the benefits
* Factors Influencing Perception: Key factors influencing community perceptions include aesthetics, perceived economic benefits, and the fairness and transparency of the planning process. Communities prefer local hiring,

procurement, and ownership, and often favor brownfield sites (like landfills) over forests or farmland for large projects

* Importance of Engagement: Effective community engagement, public consultations, and transparent communication during the planning and implementation phases are crucial for fostering acceptance and addressing concerns

3. Gender Roles and Empowerment:

* Increased Opportunities for Women: The solar industry has emerged as a significant employer of women, accounting for approximately 40% of its workforce, which is notably higher than in other renewable energy sectors. Initiatives like Barefoot College in India and Solar Sister in Africa actively train women as solar engineers (mpowerment through Access: Solar energy can reduce the time women spend on arduous tasks like collecting water or firewood, freeing them for education, economic activities, or community participation
* Addressing Gender Bias: While progress is being made, challenges such as limited access to training and financing, and occupational segregation (women often in administrative roles) still exist. Efforts are needed to promote women's leadership and equal opportunities through gender-sensitive policies and mentorship programs

Local Governance and Participation:

* Strengthening Local Governance: Solar projects can drive local governments to engage more with energy policy, promoting energy assessments, setting renewable energy targets, and creating energy efficiency programs. This fosters "local energy governance" where communities have a say in their energy future
* Community-Led Initiatives: Effective solar programs often involve collaborative efforts between local governments, community groups, civil society organizations, and private sector actors, emphasizing inclusivity and participation in decision-making).

In conclusion, solar energy programs offer immense sociological benefits, primarily through enhanced energy access, economic development, and increased social equity. However, realizing these benefits fully requires careful planning, community engagement, and policies that proactively address potential challenges like land use conflicts and ensure equitable distribution of opportunities and benefits.

The future of solar energy programs is incredibly promising, driven by rapid technological advancements, decreasing costs, and increasing global commitment to renewable energy. Here's a breakdown of key aspects:

Technological Advancements:

* Improved Solar Panel Efficiency: Ongoing research is leading to significantly higher conversion efficiencies, meaning more electricity can be generated from smaller areas. This includes:

* Perovskite Solar Cells: These are a game-changer, offering high efficiency at lower production costs. They can even be layered on top of traditional silicon cells (tandem cells) to capture more of the solar spectrum.
* Bifacial Solar Panels: These panels capture sunlight from both the front and back, increasing overall energy production.
* Thin-Film Solar Cells: Lightweight and flexible, these can be applied to various surfaces, including bendable and even transparent materials for building integration.
* Quantum Dot Solar Cells: A newer technology with potential for high efficiency and flexibility.
* Advanced Energy Storage Solutions: The intermittency of solar power is being addressed with improved battery technologies (e.g., lithium-ion, solid-state, and flow batteries) that can store excess energy for use during the night or cloudy periods.
* AI and Machine Learning: AI is revolutionizing solar by:
* Optimizing energy production and consumption in real-time.
* Improving solar energy forecasting for better grid management and energy planning.
* Predicting and minimizing solar curtailment.
* Building-Integrated Photovoltaics (BIPV): Solar panels are being seamlessly integrated into building materials like roofs, walls, and windows, offering both energy generation and aesthetic benefits.
* Floating Solar Farms: Installing solar panels on water bodies conserves land space and can even lead to higher efficiency due to cooling effects.
* Solar Tracking Systems: These systems allow panels to follow the sun's path throughout the day, maximizing energy capture.
* Night-Time Solar Plants: While still in early stages, research is exploring technologies that can generate power during the night.

1. **Decreasing Costs:**

* The cost of solar technology has fallen dramatically over the past decade, making solar installations more affordable and competitive with traditional energy sources. This trend is expected to continue with economies of scale in manufacturing.

2. **Policy and Investment Support:**

* Governments worldwide are implementing policies, incentives (like tax credits and subsidies), and ambitious renewable energy targets to accelerate solar adoption. India, for example, is a global leader in solar energy and aims to have 500 GW of renewable energy capacity by 2030, with a significant portion from solar.
* Significant foreign and domestic investments are flowing into the solar sector, driving growth and innovation.

3. Expanding Applications and Adoption:

* Rooftop Solar: This decentralized solution is gaining immense popularity for residential, commercial, and industrial buildings.
* Community Solar Programs: These allow multiple households or businesses to benefit from shared solar installations, making solar accessible to those with limited space or resources.
* Solar-Powered Transportation: Solar-powered electric vehicles and charging stations are becoming more prevalent.
* Rural Electrification: Solar energy is a viable solution for providing electricity to remote and underserved areas.
* Smart Cities: Solar energy will play a crucial role in powering urban infrastructure, smart grids, and IoT-based energy management systems.
* Solar Fuels: Research is ongoing into artificial photosynthesis to create solar fuels for energy storage and other applications.

Challenges to Overcome:

Despite the bright outlook, challenges remain, including:

* Intermittency: Managing the variability of solar output due to weather conditions. This is being addressed through improved forecasting and energy storage.
* Grid Integration: Ensuring seamless integration of large-scale solar into existing grids.
* Land Use: For large solar farms, land availability can be a concern, leading to innovations like floating solar and agrivoltaics (combining agriculture with solar).
* Supply Chain and Raw Materials: Ensuring sustainable and ethical sourcing of materials for solar panel manufacturing.

In conclusion, the future of solar energy programs is characterized by continuous innovation, increasing affordability, and widespread adoption across diverse applications. Solar is poised to become the leading source of electricity globally, playing a pivotal role in transitioning towards a clean, sustainable, and energy-independent future.

The concept of a "GDP of the universe" is not a recognized economic or scientific metric. GDP (Gross Domestic Product) is a measure of the economic activity within a defined geographical area, typically a country or region, over a specific period. It quantifies the monetary value of all finished goods and services produced and sold within that boundary.

Solar energy plays a transformative and multifaceted role in the upliftment of mankind, impacting various aspects of human well-being, economic development, and environmental sustainability. Here's how:

1. Poverty Alleviation and Economic Empowerment:

* Access to Affordable Energy: For billions globally, particularly in developing nations and rural areas, reliable electricity is a luxury. Solar power offers a decentralized, cost-effective solution, bypassing expensive grid infrastructure. This means homes can have lighting, allowing children to study after dark and improving safety.
* Reduced Energy Costs: By generating their own electricity, individuals and businesses can significantly reduce or even eliminate their reliance on expensive, often polluting, fossil fuels (like kerosene or diesel generators). This frees up household income for other necessities and makes businesses more competitive.
* Job Creation: The solar industry is a booming sector, creating jobs in manufacturing, installation, maintenance, and research. This provides stable and often higher-paying employment opportunities, particularly in regions where they are desperately needed.
* Local Economic Development: Solar mini-grids and off-grid solutions empower local communities to establish small businesses (e.g., charging stations, small shops with refrigeration, artisan workshops) that can thrive with reliable owner, leading to local economic growth and reduced migration to urban centres.
* Increased Productivity: Businesses can operate longer hours, use modern machinery, and improve efficiency with consistent power, leading to increased output and income

REFERENCES

1. MNRE Annual Reports-2021-22,22-23,23-24,24-25
2. Solar technology for 21st century by Ano Blazev ISBN 9781466582920
3. Techno-economic Analysis Edited by Konstinos Arerossis and Eleni Strantzale
4. Yale e 360 :e360.yale.ed
5. Ember :ember-ember.org
6. PV Betr :fortune.org
7. Energy Foundation China www..jchina.org
8. PV Magazene :www.pv-magazine.com
9. Denmark dk:denmark.dk
10. Nordic Energy Research:www.nordicenegy.org
11. Denmaks Tekniske :www.man.dtu.dk
12. StrategicEnergy Europe: strategicenergy.eu
13. S Energy Information:www.eia.gov

CHAPTER 4

SOLAR PV PROGRAMME IN INDIA, RELATED TECHNOLOGY, TECHNO-ECONOMIC ANALYSIS AND ITS CONTRIBUTION TO GDP OF NATION

Solar PV Programme in India

India has made significant strides in solar PV adoption, with solar energy playing a crucial role in its renewable energy targets. Here's a breakdown of the current status:

CurCrent apacity and Growth:

* As of April 30, 2025, India›s total installed solar power capacity stands at approximately 107.95 GW. This includes:
* Ground Mounted Solar Plants: 82.39 GW
* Grid-Connected Solar Rooftop: 17.69 GW
* Hybrid Projects (Solar Component): 2.89 GW
* Off-Grid Solar: 4.98 GW
* Solar energy was the biggest contributor to capacity expansion in FY 2024-25, adding 23.83 GW, a substantial increase from the previous year
* India has already surpassed the 100 GW milestone for installed solar power capacity

Targets and Goals:

* India has an ambitious target of achieving 500 GW of non-fossil fuel-based energy capacity by 2030.
* Solar power is expected to contribute nearly 300 GW to this 500 GW target, making it the leading renewable energy source.
* This aligns with India›s Nationally Determined Contributions (NDCs) under the Paris Agreement, which include cutting emissions intensity by 45% and achieving 50% non-fossil fuel capacity by 2030.

Government Policies and Initiatives

The Indian government has implemented several policies and schemes to promote solar energy adoption:

* PM Surya Ghar: Muft Bijli Yojana: This scheme aims to facilitate rooftop solar installations for households, with a significant number of installations already complete

Grid Connected Rooftop Solar Programme:

This program offers Central Financial Assistance (CFA) for rooftop solar systems, along with incentives for communal facilities in housing societies.

* PM-KUSUM Scheme:

This scheme supports farmers by solarizing agricultural practices through decentralized solar power plants, standalone solar pumps, and solarization of grid-connected agricultural pumps

* Solar Park Scheme:

This scheme focuses on developing concentrated zones for solar power generation projects.

Viability Gap Funding (VGF) Scheme: This provides financial assistance to make large-scale renewable energy projects feasible

* Production Linked Incentive (PLI) Scheme: This scheme supports domestic manufacturing of high-efficiency solar PV modules.
* Renewable Purchase Obligation (RPO): Mandates a certain percentage of electricity to be sourced from renewable energy.
* Net Metering Policies: Allow consumers to sell excess solar power back to the grid

Challenges:

Despite the impressive growth, India faces several challenges in scaling up solar PV:

* Land Acquisition: Large-scale solar farms require significant land, which can lead to conflicts with food security and environmental interests.
* Grid Integration: Integrating increasing amounts of solar power into the existing grid infrastructure can be complex and requires upgrades.
* Financing Constraints: While costs are decreasing, initial installation costs can still be substantial, especially for lower-income segments.
* Consumer Awareness and Acceptance: Many potential consumers, especially for rooftop solar, are still unaware of the benefits and available schemes.
* Regulatory Complexities and Policy Uncertainty: Inconsistent application of regulations across states, procedural delays, and occasional policy changes can hinder adoption.

* Lack of After-Sales Support: Concerns about maintenance and support services can deter consumers.
* Technical Challenges: Ensuring grid stability with multiple small solar installations and improving technical specifications for net-metering systems are ongoing challenges.

Overall, India's solar PV sector is experiencing rapid growth, driven by ambitious targets and supportive government policies. While challenges remain, the country is committed to establishing itself as a global leader in solar energy.

Solar PV Technology

Solar PV technology is a cornerstone of India's ambitious clean energy transition, demonstrating remarkable growth and holding significant future potential.

Current Status and Achievements:

* Significant Installed Capacity: As of April 2025, India has surpassed 107 GW of installed solar power capacity, with a substantial portion coming from ground-mounted plants (82.39 GW) and grid-connected rooftop solar (17.69 GW). An additional 84.10 GW is under implementation and 47.49 GW under tendering.
* Cost Reduction: The cost of solar photovoltaic modules has plummeted dramatically, by about 95%, from over Rs 200 per watt in 2010 to under Rs 9 per watt in 2024. This significant cost reduction is a key driver of India›s clean energy revolution.
* Domestic Manufacturing Growth: India›s cumulative solar module manufacturing capacity reached 64.5 GW and solar cell manufacturing capacity totaled 5.8 GW as of December 2023. These capacities are projected to surpass 150 GW and 75 GW respectively by 2026, aiming to reduce import dependence.
* Hybrid and RTC Projects: India has also seen growth in hybrid and round-the-clock (RTC) renewable energy projects, with 64.67 GW under implementation and tendered.

Latest Advancements in Solar PV Technology relevant to India:

* Increased Efficiency: Efforts are continuously underway to improve solar panel efficiency. This includes advancements in:
* PERC (Passivated Emitter and Rear Cell) technology: Enhances efficiency by capturing additional sunlight from the rear side of the panel.
* Heterojunction Solar Cells (HJT): Combining crystalline silicon and thin-film properties for higher efficiency and stability.

Emerging Technologies:

* Perovskite Solar Cells: Promising high efficiency, lower production costs, and flexibility, with breakthroughs in perovskite-silicon tandem cells achieving record efficiencies (e.g., 33.9%). They are ideal for urban infrastructure and portable energy.
* Tandem Solar Cells: Stacking multiple layers of photovoltaic materials to capture different wavelengths of sunlight, leading to higher conversion efficiencies.
* Bi -facial Solar Panels: Capturing sunlight from both sides, boosting energy yield by 10-30%, even in diffuse light conditions.
* Floating Solar Farms: Installing solar panels on water bodies, saving land, reducing water evaporation, and minimizing ecological disruptions. India is already exploring such projects in states like Kerala and Maharashtra.
* Thin-Film Solar Cells: Lightweight and flexible, applicable to various surfaces.
* Transparent Solar Panels: Integrating into windows and glass surfaces, turning buildings into power generators without blocking visibility

Integration of Smart Technologies:

* AI and IoT: Optimizing energy production and consumption by forecasting energy production, weather patterns, and real-time performance monitoring. AI is also being used for load balancing and enhancing system resilience.
* Smart Inverters: Optimizing the flow of electricity between solar panels, batteries, and the grid for efficient energy management.
* Energy Storage Solutions: Significant investment in utility-scale storage systems (e.g., lithium-ion and flow batteries) to complement solar power generation, allowing surplus energy to be stored and utilized during peak demand or low sunlight hours. India is developing around 200 GWh of battery manufacturing capacity.

Government Policies and Initiatives:

India's government has implemented several key policies and schemes to accelerate solar PV adoption and manufacturing:

* PM Surya Ghar: Muft Bijli Yojana: Launched in February 2024, this scheme provides subsidies (up to 40% for systems up to 3 kW) to households for installing rooftop solar panels, aiming to benefit 1 crore (10 million) households.
* Grid Connected Rooftop Solar Programme: Aims for 40 GW installation by 2026 with central financial assistance (CFA) for residential sectors.

* PM-KUSUM Scheme: Supports farmers by solarizing agricultural practices, including setting up decentralized solar power plants, installing standalone solar pumps, and solarizing grid-connected agricultural pumps with substantial financial aid.
* Production Linked Incentive (PLI) Scheme: Allocated significant funding to support integrated manufacturing units of high-efficiency solar PV modules, providing incentives based on sales, localization, and efficiency.
* Basic Custom Duty (BCD): Imposed on imported solar PV cells (25%) and modules (40%) to promote domestic manufacturing.
* Interstate Transmission System (ISTS) Fee Waiver: Waived for solar and wind energy sales across states for projects commissioned by June 30, 2025.
* 100% Foreign Direct Investment (FDI): Allowed through the automated process to encourage investment in the renewable energy sector.
* Standards and Labeling (S&L) Programs:

Launched by the Bureau of Energy Efficiency (BEE) for grid-connected solar inverters and PV modules to help consumers make informed choices and improve energy efficiency.

Future Outlook:

The future of solar PV technology in India is exceptionally bright, driven by:

* Ambitious Targets: India aims to achieve 500 GW of renewable energy capacity by 2030, with solar power projected to account for over 60% of this. This necessitates annual solar installations of 50-60 GW.
* Continued Cost Reductions: Further cost reductions are expected due to economies of scale in manufacturing and technological advancements.
* Technological Breakthroughs: Emerging technologies like perovskite and tandem cells, coupled with advancements in energy storage, will significantly enhance solar efficiency and reliability.
* Smart Grid Integration: AI and IoT will play a crucial role in optimizing solar power generation, storage, and distribution, leading to smarter and more resilient grids.
* Diversified Applications: Increased adoption of rooftop solar, floating solar, and Building-Integrated Photo voltaics (BIPV) will diversify solar applications.
* Geographical Advantage: India›s abundant sunlight throughout most of the year provides a natural advantage for solar power generation.

Increased Investment:

The sector is expected to attract significant foreign and domestic investment due to supportive government policies and a burgeoning market.

While challenges like land acquisition, grid integration, and the need for further infrastructure improvement exist, India's robust policy framework, technological advancements, and strong commitment to renewable energy position it as a global leader in solar PV adoption and innovation.

Techno-economic analysis of Solar Photovoltaic technology

Techno-economic analysis (TEA) of solar photovoltaic (PV) technology involves evaluating A techno both its technical performance and its economic viability. This comprehensive assessment helps determine the overall feasibility and attractiveness of solar PV systems for various applications, from residential rooftops to utility-scale power plants.

Here's a breakdown of the key aspects typically covered in a techno-economic analysis of solar PV:

I. Technical Analysis

This part focuses on the performance and characteristics of the solar PV system.

Design and Sizing:

* Determining the optimal capacity (kWp) based on energy demand, available space, and solar irradiance.
* Choosing appropriate PV module types (mono crystalline, poly crystalline, thin-film), inverters (string, micro-inverters, central), and mounting structures (fixed-tilt, single-axis tracker, dual-axis tracker).
* Considering system configuration (grid-tied, off-grid, hybrid with battery storage).
* Energy Yield Estimation:
* Simulating the expected electricity generation (kWh) using specialized software (e.g., PV Syst, SolarGIS, PVGIS) that factors in local solar irradiance, temperature, shading, module efficiency, and degradation rates.
* Analyzing the impact of panel degradation over the system›s lifespan (typically 25-30 years).
* Evaluating the benefits of solar tracking systems (20-30% more energy compared to fixed structures).
* Performance Metrics:
* Capacity Factor: The ratio of actual energy output over a period to the maximum possible output if the system operated at full rated power continuously
* Performance Ratio (PR): A measure of the actual AC output from the PV system compared to the theoretical DC output, accounting for all losses
* Efficiency: The rate at which the PV modules convert sunlight into electricity

II. Economic Analysis

This part focuses on the financial aspects of investing in and operating a solar PV system.

* Capital Expenditure (CAPEX):
* Module Cost: A significant portion of the initial investment, which has seen substantial reductions over the years.
* Inverter Cost: The cost of devices that convert DC electricity from panels to AC for household or grid use.

Balance of System (BOS) Costs: This includes:

* Mounting structures and racking.
* Cabling and electrical components (ACDB boxes, protection devices).
* Installation and labor charges.

Design, engineering, and project management.

* Permitting, inspection, and interconnection fees.
* Battery Storage Costs (if applicable): For off-grid or hybrid systems, the cost of batteries significantly impacts the overall CAPEX.
* Operational Expenditure (OPEX):
* Operations and Maintenance (O&M) Costs:
* Routine cleaning and inspections.
* Minor repairs and inverter replacements.
* Monitoring system costs.

Insurance.

* Fixed and Variable O&M Costs: Differentiated based on whether they are independent of or dependent on energy production.
* Financial Metrics:
* Levelized Cost of Energy (LCOE): This is arguably the most crucial metric, representing the average cost per unit of electricity ($/kWh or Rs./kWh) generated over the system's lifetime. It allows for a direct comparison with conventional energy sources. LCOE has been steadily declining for solar PV, making it competitive with, and often cheaper than, fossil fuels in many regions.
* Net Present Value (NPV): The present value of future cash flows minus the initial investment. A positive NPV indicates a profitable investment.

Internal Rate of Return (IRR)

The discount rate at which the NPV of all cash flows from a project equals zero. A higher IRR indicates a more desirable investment.

* Payback Period: The time it takes for the cumulative savings and revenue from the solar PV system to equal the initial investment. Both simple and discounted payback periods are often calculated.
* Return on Investment (ROI): Measures the profitability of an investment relative to its cost. Typical solar PV systems can offer an ROI of 10% to 30% or more.
* Sensitivity Analysis: Examining how changes in key variables (e.g., electricity prices, capital costs, interest rates, government incentives, inflation rates) impact the financial metrics.
* Uncertainty Assessment (e.g., Monte Carlo simulation): Quantifying the risk associated with different input variables

II. Policy and Market Factors

Government policies and market dynamics play a crucial role in the economic viability of solar PV.

* Government ncentives:
* Subsidies: Direct financial assistance for installation.
* Tax Credits/Rebates: Reductions in tax liability or direct payments.
* Feed-in Tariffs (FiTs): Guarantees a fixed price for electricity fed back into the grid.
* Net Metering: Allows solar owners to receive credit for excess electricity sent to the grid.
* Electricity Prices: The prevailing and projected electricity tariffs significantly impact the savings and revenue generated by a solar PV system. Higher retail electricity prices generally make solar more attractive.
* Market Competition: Increased competition among solar manufacturers and installers has driven down costs.
* Carbon Benefits/Environmental Externalities: While harder to quantify financially, the reduction in CO2 emissions and other pollutants from displacing fossil fuels is a significant societal benefit that can influence policy support

Current Trends and Future Outlook

* Falling Costs: The cost of solar PV has dramatically decreased over the past decade, making it one of the cheapest forms of electricity generation in many parts of the world. This trend is expected to continue.
* Increased Efficiency: Ongoing advancements in PV technology are leading to higher module efficiencies.

* Integration with Storage: The growing adoption of battery energy storage systems (BESS) alongside PV is enhancing grid stability, enabling greater self-consumption, and increasing the economic viability of solar, especially in regions with time-of-use tariffs or unreliable grids.
* «Solar PV Rooftop as a Service» (RaaS): Emerging business models where providers install and maintain PV systems on rooftops, offering electricity to consumers as a service, without the upfront investment.
* Decentralized Generation: Solar PV is a cornerstone of distributed generation, empowering consumers to become prosumers and reducing reliance on centralized power grids.

In conclusion, techno-economic analysis is essential for understanding the holistic value proposition of solar PV technology. It provides a robust framework for investors, policymakers, and consumers to make informed decisions about adopting solar energy, considering both its technical performance and its compelling economic advantages.

Solar PV technology is a cornerstone of India's ambitious clean energy transition, demonstrating remarkable growth and holding significant future potential.

Current Status and Achievements:

* Significant Installed Capacity: As of April 2025, India has surpassed 107 GW of installed solar power capacity, with a substantial portion coming from ground-mounted plants (82.39 GW) and grid-connected rooftop solar (17.69 GW). An additional 84.10 GW is under implementation and 47.49 GW under tendering.
* Cost Reduction: The cost of solar photovoltaic modules has plummeted dramatically, by about 95%, from over Rs 200 per watt in 2010 to under Rs 9 per watt in 2024. This significant cost reduction is a key driver of India›s clean energy revolution.
* Domestic Manufacturing Growth: India›s cumulative solar module manufacturing capacity reached 64.5 GW and solar cell manufacturing capacity totaled 5.8 GW as of December 2023. These capacities are projected to surpass 150 GW and 75 GW respectively by 2026, aiming to reduce import dependence.
* Hybrid and RTC Projects: India has also seen growth in hybrid and round-the-clock (RTC) renewable energy projects, with 64.67 GW under implementation and tendered.

Latest Advancements in Solar PV Technology relevant to India:

* Increased Efficiency: Efforts are continuously underway to improve solar panel efficiency. This includes advancements in:
* PERC (Passivated Emitter and Rear Cell) technology: Enhances efficiency by capturing additional sunlight from the rear side of the panel.

* Heterojunction Solar Cells (HJT): Combining crystalline silicon and thin-film properties for higher efficiency and stability.
* Emerging Technologies:
* Perovskite Solar Cells: Promising high efficiency, lower production costs, and flexibility, with breakthroughs in perovskite-silicon tandem cells achieving record efficiencies (e.g., 33.9%). They are ideal for urban infrastructure and portable energy.
* Tandem Solar Cells: Stacking multiple layers of photovoltaic materials to capture different wavelengths of sunlight, leading to higher conversion efficiencies.
* Bifacial Solar Panels: Capturing sunlight from both sides, boosting energy yield by 10-30%, even in diffuse light conditions.
* Floating Solar Farms: Installing solar panels on water bodies, saving land, reducing water evaporation, and minimizing ecological disruptions. India is already exploring such projects in states like Kerala and Maharashtra.
* Thin-Film Solar Cells: Lightweight and flexible, applicable to various surfaces.
* Transparent Solar Panels: Integrating into windows and glass surfaces, turning buildings into power generators without blocking visibility.

Integration of Smart Technologies:

* AI and IoT: Optimizing energy production and consumption by forecasting energy production, weather patterns, and real-time performance monitoring. AI is also being used for load balancing and enhancing system resilience.
* Smart Inverters: Optimizing the flow of electricity between solar panels, batteries, and the grid for efficient energy management.
* Energy Storage Solutions: Significant investment in utility-scale storage systems (e.g., lithium-ion and flow batteries) to complement solar power generation, allowing surplus energy to be stored and utilized during peak demand or low sunlight hours. India is developing around 200 GWh of battery manufacturing capacity.

Government Policies and Initiatives:

India's government has implemented several key policies and schemes to accelerate solar PV adoption and manufacturing:

* PM Surya Ghar: Muft Bijli Yojana: Launched in February 2024, this scheme provides subsidies (up to 40% for systems up to 3 kW) to households for installing rooftop solar panels, aiming to benefit 1 crore (10 million) households.
* Grid Connected Rooftop Solar Programme: Aims for 40 GW installation by 2026 with central financial assistance (CFA) for residential sectors.

* PM-KUSUM Scheme: Supports farmers by solarizing agricultural practices, including setting up decentralized solar power plants, installing standalone solar pumps, and solarizing grid-connected agricultural pumps with substantial financial aid.
* Production Linked Incentive (PLI) Scheme: Allocated significant funding to support integrated manufacturing units of high-efficiency solar PV modules, providing incentives based on sales, localization, and efficiency.
* Basic Custom Duty (BCD): Imposed on imported solar PV cells (25%) and modules (40%) to promote domestic manufacturing.
* Interstate Transmission System (ISTS) Fee Waiver: Waived for solar and wind energy sales across states for projects commissioned by June 30, 2025.
* 100% Foreign Direct Investment (FDI): Allowed through the automated process to encourage investment in the renewable energy sector.
* Standards and Labeling (S&L) Programs: Launched by the Bureau of Energy Efficiency (BEE) for grid-connected solar inverters and PV modules to help consumers make informed choices and improve energy efficiency.

Future Outlook:

The future of solar PV technology in India is exceptionally bright, driven by:

* Ambitious Targets: India aims to achieve 500 GW of renewable energy capacity by 2030, with solar power projected to account for over 60% of this. This necessitates annual solar installations of 50-60 GW.
* Continued Cost Reductions: Further cost reductions are expected due to economies of scale in manufacturing and technological advancements.
* Technological Breakthroughs: Emerging technologies like perovskite and tandem cells, coupled with advancements in energy storage, will significantly enhance solar efficiency and reliability.
* Smart Grid Integration:

AI and IoT will play a crucial role in optimizing solar power generation, storage, and distribution, leading to smarter and more resilient grids.

* Diversified Applications: Increased adoption of rooftop solar, floating solar, and Building-Integrated Photovoltaics (BIPV) will diversify solar applications.
* Geographical Advantage: India›s abundant sunlight throughout most of the year provides a natural advantage for solar power generation.
* Increased Investment: The sector is expected to attract significant foreign and domestic investment due to supportive government policies and a burgeoning market.

While challenges like land acquisition, grid integration, and the need for further infrastructure improvement exist, India's robust policy framework, technological advancements, and strong commitment to renewable energy position it as a global leader in solar PV adoption and innovation.

Contritbuionola of SPV Programme in GDP of India

Solar PV technology is making a significant and multifaceted contribution to India's GDP, touching various sectors of the economy. Here's a breakdown of how:

* Direct Economic Contribution (Market Size & Investment):
* Growing Market: India›s solar energy market is expanding rapidly, projected to reach USD 24.9 billion by 2030 (from USD 10.4 billion in 2023), with a Compound Annual Growth Rate (CAGR) of 13.4%. This direct market value is a clear contributor to GDP.
* Massive Investment: The sector attracts substantial investment, both domestic and foreign. Foreign capital invested in India›s solar power projects was nearly US$20.7 billion between 2010 and 2019, and India received US$3.76 billion in foreign capital in FY2023-24. This investment directly fuels economic activity.
* Manufacturing Growth: India›s solar manufacturing capabilities are booming. Solar module production capacity jumped from a modest 2 GW in 2014 to 90 GW in 2024, with projections estimating 150 GW by 2030. This domestic manufacturing contributes to industrial output and value addition within the country.
* Job Creation and Employment:
* Significant Workforce: The solar PV sector is a major employment generator. In 2023, India›s solar PV sector employed about 318,600 people in both on-grid and off-grid systems.
* Rapid Job Growth: India›s solar workforce has expanded by 165% over the last 5 years. IRENA estimates that India had 238,000 jobs in grid-connected solar PV in 2023, an 18% increase from 2022.
* Diverse Opportunities: Jobs are created across the entire value chain, including manufacturing, engineering, project development, construction, installation, sales, and maintenance of PV systems.
* Higher Wages: Average monthly salaries in solar are roughly 20% higher than economy-wide averages, indicating a positive impact on disposable income and living standards.
* Rural Electrification and Livelihoods: Off-grid solar solutions, particularly in rural areas, improve quality of life and enable schools, hospitals, and commercial enterprises to function efficiently, indirectly boosting local economies. The PM-KUSUM Scheme alone is estimated to generate employment opportunities equivalent to 7.55 lakh job-years.
* Cost Savings and Enhanced Competitiveness:
* Reduced Electricity Bills: For households and businesses, on-site electricity generation from solar PV significantly reduces electricity bills. This frees up capital that can be used for other investments or consumption, stimulating economic activity.

* Lower Industrial Costs: Reduced electricity costs for industries can enhance their competitiveness, lower operational expenses, and potentially lead to increased production and job creation.
* Reduced Government Expenditure: Schemes promoting solar power, such as PM Surya Ghar Muft Bijli Yojana, are expected to save the government an estimated ₹75,000 crore annually in electricity costs by promoting widespread solar adoption.
* Energy Security and Reduced Imports: By generating electricity domestically from solar, India reduces its reliance on imported fossil fuels, which contributes to a better trade balance and enhances energy security. India›s net energy import bill is currently about 3% of GDP, and increasing renewable energy can reduce this.
* Enabling Growth in Other Sectors:
* Infrastructure Development: The growth of solar projects necessitates the development of supporting infrastructure, including battery storage, inverters, and grid stabilization devices, further stimulating industrial growth and supporting «Make in India» efforts.
* Agricultural Boost: Solar water pumps and cold storage facilities for agriculture, powered by solar, can reduce food wastage and boost agricultural productivity, leading to increased income for farmers and supporting the rural economy.
* Meeting Climate Targets and Attracting Green Investment:
* While not a direct GDP contribution, meeting ambitious renewable energy targets (like 500 GW by 2030, with a significant portion from solar) positions India as a global leader in clean energy. This attracts further green investments and fosters innovation, creating a positive feedback loop for long-term economic growth.
* Clean energy contributed slightly less than 5% of India›s GDP growth in 2023, predominantly from investment in new solar power capacity. This highlights the substantial role of clean energy, especially solar, in driving overall economic expansion.

In essence, solar PV technology contributes to India's GDP through direct investments, job creation, manufacturing, cost savings for consumers and industries, reduced import bills, and by enabling broader economic growth through enhanced energy security and sustainable Srong impetus to its economic growth.

REFERENCES

1. MNRE Annual Reports-2021-22,2022-23,2023-24,and2024-25
2. Solar Photovoltaic -Fundamentals-Technologies and Applications ,C.S.Negi,PHI learning
3. Department of Energy www.energy.gov
4. American Solar Energy ases.org
5. infolink www.infolink-group.com
6. V S Energy Information www.eia.gov

7. Raisin www.raisin.com
8. Solar Energy World www.solarenergyword.com
9. IEA International Energy www.iea.org
10. The United Nations www.un.org

CHAPTER 5

SOLAR THERMAL ENERGY TECHNOLOGY THEIR TECHNO-ECONOMIC ANALYSIS EFFECT ON ENVIRONMENT AND CLIMATE CHANGE MITIGATION AND CONTRIBUTION TO GDP OF NATION

Introduction

Solar thermal technology harnesses the sun's energy to generate heat, which can then be used for various purposes, including electricity generation, water heating, and space heating/cooling. Unlike photovoltaic (PV) systems that convert sunlight directly into electricity, solar thermal systems focus on capturing and utilizing the sun's thermal energy.

Principles of Solar Thermal Technology:

The fundamental principle behind solar thermal technology involves collecting and concentrating solar radiation to increase the temperature of a heat-transfer fluid. This process often utilizes the "greenhouse effect," where a reflective surface transmits short-wave radiation (sunlight) and traps the resulting long-wave infrared radiation (heat) within the collector.

Key principles include:

* Heat Gain: Accumulating heat from the sun within the system.
* Heat Transfer: Moving the absorbed heat from the collector to a heat-transfer fluid (e.g., water, oil). This occurs through conduction and convection.
* Heat Storage: Storing the collected heat in a thermal energy storage system (e.g., insulated tanks with water, molten salts, rocks) for later use, especially during periods without sunlight.
* Heat Transport: Circulating the heated fluid from the collector to the storage system or directly to the point of use.

* Heat Insulation: Preventing heat loss from collectors, transport tubing, and storage units to maintain efficiency.

Solar Thermal Technologies:

Types of Technologies

Solar thermal technologies are broadly classified by the temperature range they achieve and whether they concentrate sunlight:

1. Non-Concentrating Collectors (Low to Medium Temperature):

* Flat-Plate Collectors: These are common for domestic hot water and space heating. They consist of a dark absorber plate, usually with copper pipes, covered by a transparent glazing and insulated on the back. They work on the greenhouse effect, heating a fluid that circulates through the pipes.
* Evacuated Tube Collectors (ETCs): These are more efficient than flat-plate collectors, especially in cooler climates. They consist of multiple glass tubes, each containing a heat-absorbing fin and a heat pipe, with a vacuum between the two glass layers to minimize heat loss.
* Unglazed Solar Collectors: Simple systems, often dark metal or plastic, that absorb sunlight and transfer heat to a fluid. Commonly used for swimming pool heating due to their lower temperature requirements.
* Transpired Solar Air Collectors: Used to pre-heat ventilation air for buildings. Air flows through a perforated dark absorber material, absorbing heat from the sun.

2. Concentrating Solar Power (CSP) Systems (High Temperature):
These systems use mirrors or lenses to concentrate sunlight onto a small area, achieving much higher temperatures suitable for electricity generation and industrial process heat. They typically include tracking systems to follow the sun's movement.

* Parabolic Trough Systems: Long, U-shaped mirrors focus sunlight onto a receiver tube running along the focal line. A heat-transfer fluid circulates through the tube, gets heated, and then is used to generate steam for a turbine.
* Solar Power Towers (Central Receiver Systems): Hundreds or thousands of large, sun-tracking mirrors (heliostats) reflect and concentrate sunlight onto a central receiver atop a tower. The concentrated sunlight heats a fluid (e.g., molten salt) in the receiver to very high temperatures, which then generates steam for electricity.
* Solar Dish/Engine Systems: Parabolic dish-shaped mirrors concentrate sunlight onto a receiver at the dish's focal point, where a Stirling engine (or similar heat engine) directly converts the heat into mechanical energy to drive a generator.

* Linear Fresnel Reflectors: A series of long, flat or slightly curved mirrors arranged in parallel rows focus sunlight onto a receiver tube mounted above them. This design can be more cost-effective than parabolic troughs.

Applications of Solar Thermal Technology:

Solar thermal technology has a wide range of applications across residential, commercial, and industrial sectors:

* Domestic Hot Water (DHW) Heating: One of the most common applications, significantly reducing reliance on conventional water heaters.
* Space Heating and Cooling: Providing heat for buildings during colder months and enabling solar thermal cooling (e.g., absorption chillers) in warmer climates.
* Swimming Pool Heating: A simple and effective way to extend the swimming season and reduce heating costs.
* Industrial Process Heat: Supplying heat for various industrial processes that require moderate to high temperatures, such as food processing, chemical production, and textile manufacturing.
* Electricity Generation (CSP): Large-scale solar thermal power plants generate electricity by using concentrated solar heat to produce steam that drives turbines.
* Solar Cooking: Using concentrated solar energy for cooking food, especially in off-grid or remote areas.
* Solar Distillation and Desalination: Utilizing solar heat to purify water or desalt seawater.
* Agricultural Drying: Drying crops, fruits, and vegetables using solar-heated air.

Advantages of Solar Thermal Technology:

* Renewable and Sustainable: Utilizes an inexhaustible energy source – the sun.
* Reduces Electricity Bills: Lowers energy costs by supplementing or replacing conventional heating methods.
* Diverse Applications: Versatile for various heating, cooling, and power generation needs.
* Environmental Benefits: Produces no greenhouse gas emissions during operation, contributing to cleaner air.
* Thermal Energy Storage: CSP systems can incorporate thermal energy storage, allowing for continuous power generation even after sunset or during cloudy periods, enhancing reliability and dispatchability.
* Lower Operating Costs: Once installed, solar thermal systems have relatively low ongoing operational costs.

Disadvantages of Solar Thermal Technology:

* High Initial Capital Cost: The upfront investment for solar thermal systems, particularly large-scale CSP plants, can be substantial.
* Intermittency/Weather Dependence: Performance is affected by weather conditions (cloud cover, rain) and the time of day, as sunlight is required.
* Space Requirements: Large-scale CSP plants require significant land areas, typically in arid or desert regions with high solar insolation.
* Water Usage (for CSP): Some CSP technologies, especially those using steam turbines, require water for cooling, which can be a challenge in arid areas.
* Efficiency in Winter/Low Sunlight: Non-concentrating systems may be less efficient in winter or during periods of low solar radiation.
* Not Cost-Competitive with PV (for electricity): For electricity generation, CSP has generally struggled to compete on cost with solar PV in recent years, though its storage capabilities offer unique advantages.

Solar thermal technology is a method of harnessing energy from the sun to generate heat. Unlike solar photovoltaic (PV) systems, which convert sunlight directly into electricity, solar thermal systems use solar radiation to heat a fluid, which can then be used for a variety of purposes.

How it Works

The fundamental principle of solar thermal technology is the use of a solar collector to capture the sun's energy. This energy is absorbed by a black surface and transferred to a fluid (like water, air, or a heat-transfer fluid). The heated fluid is then used for different applications.

Solar thermal collectors are typically classified into three categories based on the temperature they can achieve:

* Low-temperature collectors: These are used for applications that require lower temperatures, such as residential solar water heaters. The most common type is the flat-plate collector, which consists of an insulated box with a dark absorber plate and a glass cover.
* Medium-temperature collectors: These are used for heating water or air for residential and commercial purposes. They can achieve higher temperatures than low-temperature collectors and are often used for space heating and industrial processes.
* High-temperature collectors: These systems concentrate sunlight using mirrors or lenses to achieve very high temperatures (up to 400°C or more). They are primarily used for generating electricity in solar thermal power plants, also known as Concentrating Solar-Thermal Power (CSP) systems.

Types of Concentrating Solar-Thermal Power (CSP) Systems

For large-scale electricity generation, high-temperature collectors are used in several different configurations:

* Parabolic Troughs: These systems use long, curved, trough-shaped mirrors to focus sunlight onto a receiver tube running along the mirror›s focal line. A fluid is heated as it flows through the tube, and this heat is used to produce steam, which drives a turbine to generate electricity.
* Solar Power Towers: In this configuration, a large field of sun-tracking mirrors (heliostats) concentrates sunlight onto a receiver at the top of a central tower. The concentrated sunlight heats a fluid, which is then used to create steam for a turbine.
* Dish/Engine Systems: These systems use a parabolic dish to focus sunlight onto a receiver located at the dish›s focal point. An engine, such as a Stirling engine, is attached to the receiver and uses the heat to produce electricity.

Applications of Solar Thermal Technology

Solar thermal technology has a wide range of applications, from small-scale residential use to large-scale industrial processes:

* Domestic Hot Water: This is one of the most common applications. Solar water heaters can provide a significant portion of a household›s hot water needs, reducing reliance on conventional energy sources like electricity or gas.
* Space Heating and Cooling: Solar thermal systems can be used to provide heat for buildings and even to power absorption chillers for air conditioning.
* Industrial Process Heat: Many industrial processes, such as food and beverage production, chemical manufacturing, and petroleum refining, require significant amounts of heat. Solar thermal can be used to meet these energy demands, helping to decarbonize the industrial sector.
* Electricity Generation (CSP): As described above, high-temperature solar thermal systems are used in power plants to generate utility-scale electricity. These plants often include thermal energy storage, which allows them to continue producing electricity even when the sun is not shining.

A solar thermal device, often referred to as a solar water heater, works by converting sunlight into heat to warm water or a heat transfer fluid. While the specific design can vary (e.g., flat plate vs. evacuated tube, active vs. passive systems), the core components remain similar.

Here are the main parts of a typical solar thermal system:

* Solar Collectors: This is the heart of the system, responsible for absorbing solar radiation and converting it into heat. There are two primary types:
* Flat Plate Collectors: These consist of an insulated box with a transparent cover (glass or plastic) and a dark-colored absorber plate inside. Water or a heat transfer fluid flows through

tubes attached to the absorber plate, getting heated as it passes through. They are robust and good for moderate temperatures.

* Evacuated Tube Collectors (ETCs): These are made of multiple glass tubes with a vacuum between two layers of glass. This vacuum acts as an excellent insulator, significantly reducing heat loss and making ETCs more efficient, especially in colder climates or when higher temperatures are desired. Inside each tube, there›s typically an absorber fin or a heat pipe that transfers heat to a manifold.
* Storage Tank (Hot Water Tank): This insulated tank stores the hot water heated by the solar collectors.
* It›s designed to minimize heat loss, often with thick insulation.
* For indirect systems, it will contain a heat exchanger coil through which the heated fluid from the collectors circulates, transferring its heat to the potable water in the tank without mixing.
* It often includes an auxiliary heating element (electric or gas) to provide hot water when solar input is insufficient (e.g., cloudy days or high demand).
* Heat Transfer Fluid: This fluid circulates through the solar collectors to absorb heat.
* In direct systems, potable water itself is heated directly in the collectors and then sent to the storage tank.
* In indirect (closed-loop) systems, a specialized heat transfer fluid (often a non-toxic propylene glycol-water mixture for freeze protection) circulates through the collectors and then through a heat exchanger in the storage tank to transfer its heat to the potable water.
* Piping/Plumbing: A network of insulated pipes connects the solar collectors to the storage tank and then to the building›s hot water distribution system. Proper insulation is crucial to minimize heat loss during transfer.
* Circulation Pump (for Active Systems): In active solar thermal systems, a pump is used to circulate the heat transfer fluid between the solar collectors and the storage tank.
* Controller (Solar Differential Temperature Controller): This electronic device monitors the temperature in the solar collectors and the storage tank. It activates the circulation pump only when the temperature in the collectors is significantly higher than the temperature in the tank, ensuring efficient heat collection and preventing heat loss from the tank to the collectors.
* Expansion Tank: This tank accommodates the thermal expansion of the heat transfer fluid in the closed solar loop as it heats up. It prevents excessive pressure buildup in the system.
* Safety Valves (Pressure Relief Valves): These are crucial safety devices that automatically open to release excess pressure in the system, preventing damage to components.
* Air Vents (Air Purging Valves): Installed at high points in the piping, these allow air to be purged from the system during filling and operation, ensuring proper fluid circulation.
* Mounting Structure/Frame: This provides a stable and angled support for the solar collectors, typically on a roof or a ground-mounted rack, optimizing their exposure to the sun.

* Anode Rod (for Storage Tank): In many storage tanks, an anode rod is present to protect the tank from corrosion through cathodic protection.

These components work together to efficiently capture solar energy and convert it into usable heat for various applications, most commonly hot water for domestic, commercial, or industrial use.

Installing a solar thermal plant is a detailed process that involves several key stages, from initial planning to commissioning and ongoing maintenance. Unlike solar PV (photovoltaic) systems that generate electricity, solar thermal systems primarily produce heat for various applications like water heating, space heating, or even power generation (Concentrated Solar Power - CSP).

Here's a comprehensive guide to the installation of a solar thermal plant:

1. Planning and Feasibility Study
   Before any physical installation begins, thorough planning is crucial.

* Assess Energy Needs: Determine the amount of hot water or heat required. This will dictate the size and type of solar thermal system needed. For example, a household will have different needs than a commercial or industrial application.
* Site Assessment:
* Location: Identify an area that receives ample, unobstructed direct sunlight throughout the day. For rooftop installations, assess the roofs orientation (south-facing is generally ideal in the Northern Hemisphere) and pitch. For ground-mounted systems, consider land availability and proximity to the building where heat will be used.
* Shading Analysis: Identify and address any potential shading from trees, buildings, or other structures that could reduce system efficiency.
* Structural Integrity: For rooftop installations, ensure the roof can support the weight of the collectors and associated equipment.
* Proximity: The closer the collectors are to the storage tank and heat demand, the more efficient the system will be due to minimized heat loss in pipes.
* System Sizing: Based on energy needs and site assessment, calculate the appropriate size of the solar collectors and the hot water storage tank.
* Storage Tank: Typically, 15-20 gallons per person per day or per bedroom is a rough estimate for domestic hot water.
* Solar Collectors: Approximately 0.5 to 1 sq/ft of solar panels per gallon of storage is a general guideline.
* Choose Technology:
* Flat Plate Collectors: Common for residential and small commercial applications, good for moderate temperatures.

* Evacuated Tube Collectors: More efficient in colder climates or when higher temperatures are required.
* Concentrating Solar Power (CSP): Used for large-scale power generation, involving mirrors (parabolic troughs, power towers, dish/engine systems) to concentrate sunlight.
* Permits and Regulations: Research and obtain all necessary permits and approvals from local authorities, zoning boards, and building departments. This often includes environmental clearances, grid connectivity agreements (if applicable for CSP), and construction permits.
* Budget and Financing: Develop a detailed budget, including equipment, installation, and potential ongoing maintenance costs. Explore available subsidies, incentives, or financing options.
* Professional Consultation: Engage with authorized and experienced solar thermal installers or engineers. They can provide expert advice, conduct detailed assessments, and ensure compliance with standards.

2. Component Procurement

Acquire all necessary components based on the system design:

* Solar Collectors: Flat plate, evacuated tube, or concentrating collectors.
* Storage Tank: Insulated hot water storage tank, often specifically designed for solar thermal systems with multiple coils for heat exchange.
* Heat Exchanger: (If not integrated into the storage tank) Facilitates heat transfer from the collector›s fluid to the potable water or other heating medium.
* Piping: Insulated pipes suitable for high temperatures and the specific heat transfer fluid.
* Heat Transfer Fluid: Typically a glycol-water mixture for freeze protection in colder climates, or simply water in warmer regions.
* Circulation Pump: To circulate the heat transfer fluid between the collectors and the storage tank.
* Controller: A solar differential temperature controller that monitors temperatures in the collectors and the storage tank, activating the pump when heat can be collected.
* Expansion Tank: Accommodates the thermal expansion of the heat transfer fluid.
* Pressure Relief Valves and Air Vents: Safety devices to release excess pressure and purge air from the system.
* Mounting Hardware: Racks, brackets, and fasteners suitable for the roof or ground installation.
* Instrumentation: Temperature and pressure gauges, flow meters for monitoring.
* Auxiliary Heating System: Often integrated to provide heat when solar input is insufficient (e.g., a conventional water heater or boiler).

3. Installation Process

The installation sequence can vary slightly depending on the system type, but generally follows these steps:

* Site Preparation: Clear the installation area, ensure safe access (e.g., erect scaffolding for roof work), and protect the surrounding environment.
* Mounting Structure Installation:
* Roof-mounted: Secure mounting brackets and rails to the roof rafters, ensuring proper flashing and sealing of all roof penetrations to prevent leaks. The structure should be angled correctly to maximize solar exposure.
* Ground-mounted: Install a stable foundation and secure the mounting racks.
* Collector Installation: Carefully lift and secure the solar collectors onto the mounting structure. Ensure they are aligned correctly and firmly fastened.
* Piping and Plumbing:
* Primary Loop (Solar Circuit): Run insulated pipes from the collectors to the storage tank (or heat exchanger). Ensure proper sloping for drainage and air purging.
* Secondary Loop (Hot Water/Load Circuit): Connect the heat exchanger or storage tank to the building›s hot water system or other heating loads.
* Valves and Sensors: Install shut-off valves, check valves, pressure relief valves, air vents, and temperature/pressure sensors at appropriate points in the system.
* Storage Tank Installation: Position and secure the hot water storage tank, making necessary plumbing connections to the solar circuit and the building›s water supply.
* Pump and Controller Installation: Install the circulation pump(s) and the solar controller, wiring them according to manufacturer instructions. The controller will manage the pump operation based on temperature differentials.
* Electrical Wiring: For pumps, controllers, and any auxiliary heating elements, complete all necessary electrical wiring according to local codes. Ensure proper grounding.
* Integration with Auxiliary System: Connect the solar thermal system to any existing auxiliary heating system (e.g., boiler, electric water heater) to ensure a continuous supply of hot water or heat.

4. Commissioning

This critical phase ensures the system is operating correctly and safely.

* Flushing the Solar Circuit: Thoroughly flush the solar circuit to remove any debris, air, or impurities.
* Leak Testing: Pressurize the system and meticulously check all connections, pipes, and components for any leaks. Rectify any leaks immediately.

* Filling with Heat Transfer Fluid: Fill the solar circuit with the appropriate heat transfer fluid (e.g., glycol-water mixture) to the correct pressure.
* Setting Pump and Controller: Configure the pump and controller settings according to the system design and manufacturer specifications. This includes setting temperature differentials for pump activation.
* System Test and Operation:
* Start the system and monitor its operation.
* Verify that the pump is circulating fluid, the collectors are heating up, and heat is being transferred to the storage tank.
* Check temperatures at various points to ensure efficient heat collection.
* Confirm the proper functioning of all sensors, valves, and safety devices.
* Documentation and Handover: Provide the owner with all manuals, warranties, and a detailed explanation of system operation, maintenance requirements, and troubleshooting tips.

5. Maintenance and Monitoring

   Regular maintenance is essential for optimal performance and longevity.

* Routine Checks: Periodically inspect collectors for dirt, dust, or damage. Clean collectors as needed.
* Fluid Levels and Quality: Check the heat transfer fluid level and condition. Top up or replace as necessary.
* Pump and Valve Inspection: Ensure pumps are operating smoothly and valves are functioning correctly.
* System Performance Monitoring: Monitor energy output, temperatures, and overall system efficiency. Many systems come with monitoring software or displays.
* Professional Servicing: Schedule periodic professional inspections and maintenance.

By following these steps, you can ensure a successful installation and efficient operation of a solar thermal plant. Always prioritize safety and consult with qualified professionals throughout the process.

Installing a solar thermal plant is a detailed process that involves several key stages, from initial planning to commissioning and ongoing maintenance. Unlike solar PV (photovoltaic) systems that generate electricity, solar thermal systems primarily produce heat for various applications like water heating, space heating, or even power generation (Concentrated Solar Power - CSP).

Here's a comprehensive guide to the installation of a solar thermal plant:

1. Planning and Feasibility Study

   Before any physical installation begins, thorough planning is crucial.

* Assess Energy Needs: Determine the amount of hot water or heat required. This will dictate the size and type of solar thermal system needed. For example, a household will have different needs than a commercial or industrial application.
* Site Assessment:
* Location: Identify an area that receives ample, unobstructed direct sunlight throughout the day. For rooftop installations, assess the roof›s orientation (south-facing is generally ideal in the Northern Hemisphere) and pitch. For ground-mounted systems, consider land availability and proximity to the building where heat will be used.
* Shading Analysis: Identify and address any potential shading from trees, buildings, or other structures that could reduce system efficiency.
* Structural Integrity: For rooftop installations, ensure the roof can support the weight of the collectors and associated equipment.
* Proximity: The closer the collectors are to the storage tank and heat demand, the more efficient the system will be due to minimized heat loss in pipes.
* System Sizing: Based on energy needs and site assessment, calculate the appropriate size of the solar collectors and the hot water storage tank.
* Storage Tank: Typically, 15-20 gallons per person per day or per bedroom is a rough estimate for domestic hot water.
* Solar Collectors: Approximately 0.5 to 1 sq/ft of solar panels per gallon of storage is a general guideline.
* Choose Technology:
* Flat Plate Collectors: Common for residential and small commercial applications, good for moderate temperatures.
* Evacuated Tube Collectors: More efficient in colder climates or when higher temperatures are required.
* Concentrating Solar Power (CSP): Used for large-scale power generation, involving mirrors (parabolic troughs, power towers, dish/engine systems) to concentrate sunlight.
* Permits and Regulations: Research and obtain all necessary permits and approvals from local authorities, zoning boards, and building departments. This often includes environmental clearances, grid connectivity agreements (if applicable for CSP), and construction permits.
* Budget and Financing: Develop a detailed budget, including equipment, installation, and potential ongoing maintenance costs. Explore available subsidies, incentives, or financing options.
* Professional Consultation: Engage with authorized and experienced solar thermal installers or engineers. They can provide expert advice, conduct detailed assessments, and ensure compliance with standards.

2. Component Procurement

Acquire all necessary components based on the system design:

* Solar Collectors: Flat plate, evacuated tube, or concentrating collectors.
* Storage Tank: Insulated hot water storage tank, often specifically designed for solar thermal systems with multiple coils for heat exchange.
* Heat Exchanger: (If not integrated into the storage tank) Facilitates heat transfer from the collector›s fluid to the potable water or other heating medium.
* Piping: Insulated pipes suitable for high temperatures and the specific heat transfer fluid.
* Heat Transfer Fluid: Typically a glycol-water mixture for freeze protection in colder climates, or simply water in warmer regions.
* Circulation Pump: To circulate the heat transfer fluid between the collectors and the storage tank.
* Controller: A solar differential temperature controller that monitors temperatures in the collectors and the storage tank, activating the pump when heat can be collected.
* Expansion Tank: Accommodates the thermal expansion of the heat transfer fluid.
* Pressure Relief Valves and Air Vents: Safety devices to release excess pressure and purge air from the system.
* Mounting Hardware: Racks, brackets, and fasteners suitable for the roof or ground installation.
* Instrumentation: Temperature and pressure gauges, flow meters for monitoring.
* Auxiliary Heating System: Often integrated to provide heat when solar input is insufficient (e.g., a conventional water heater or boiler).

3. Installation Process

The installation sequence can vary slightly depending on the system type, but generally follows these steps:

* Site Preparation: Clear the installation area, ensure safe access (e.g., erect scaffolding for roof work), and protect the surrounding environment.
* Mounting Structure Installation:
* Roof-mounted: Secure mounting brackets and rails to the roof rafters, ensuring proper flashing and sealing of all roof penetrations to prevent leaks. The structure should be angled correctly to maximize solar exposure.
* Ground-mounted: Install a stable foundation and secure the mounting racks.
* Collector Installation: Carefully lift and secure the solar collectors onto the mounting structure. Ensure they are aligned correctly and firmly fastened.
* Piping and Plumbing:
* Primary Loop (Solar Circuit): Run insulated pipes from the collectors to the storage tank (or heat exchanger). Ensure proper sloping for drainage and air purging.

* Secondary Loop (Hot Water/Load Circuit): Connect the heat exchanger or storage tank to the building›s hot water system or other heating loads.
* Valves and Sensors: Install shut-off valves, check valves, pressure relief valves, air vents, and temperature/pressure sensors at appropriate points in the system.
* Storage Tank Installation: Position and secure the hot water storage tank, making necessary plumbing connections to the solar circuit and the building›s water supply.
* Pump and Controller Installation: Install the circulation pump(s) and the solar controller, wiring them according to manufacturer instructions. The controller will manage the pump operation based on temperature differentials.
* Electrical Wiring: For pumps, controllers, and any auxiliary heating elements, complete all necessary electrical wiring according to local codes. Ensure proper grounding.
* Integration with Auxiliary System: Connect the solar thermal system to any existing auxiliary heating system (e.g., boiler, electric water heater) to ensure a continuous supply of hot water or heat.

4. Commissioning

   This critical phase ensures the system is operating correctly and safely.

* Flushing the Solar Circuit: Thoroughly flush the solar circuit to remove any debris, air, or impurities.
* Leak Testing: Pressurize the system and meticulously check all connections, pipes, and components for any leaks. Rectify any leaks immediately.
* Filling with Heat Transfer Fluid: Fill the solar circuit with the appropriate heat transfer fluid (e.g., glycol-water mixture) to the correct pressure.
* Setting Pump and Controller: Configure the pump and controller settings according to the system design and manufacturer specifications. This includes setting temperature differentials for pump activation.
* System Test and Operation:
* Start the system and monitor its operation.
* Verify that the pump is circulating fluid, the collectors are heating up, and heat is being transferred to the storage tank.
* Check temperatures at various points to ensure efficient heat collection.
* Confirm the proper functioning of all sensors, valves, and safety devices.
* Documentation and Handover: Provide the owner with all manuals, warranties, and a detailed explanation of system operation, maintenance requirements, and troubleshooting tips.

5. Maintenance and Monitoring

   Regular maintenance is essential for optimal performance and longevity.

* Routine Checks: Periodically inspect collectors for dirt, dust, or damage. Clean collectors as needed.
* Fluid Levels and Quality: Check the heat transfer fluid level and condition. Top up or replace as necessary.
* Pump and Valve Inspection: Ensure pumps are operating smoothly and valves are functioning correctly.
* System Performance Monitoring: Monitor energy output, temperatures, and overall system efficiency. Many systems come with monitoring software or displays.
* Professional Servicing: Schedule periodic professional inspections and maintenance.

By following these steps, you can ensure a successful installation and efficient operation of a solar thermal plant. Always prioritize safety and consult with qualified professionals throughout the process.

Installing a solar thermal plant is a detailed process that involves several key stages, from initial planning to commissioning and ongoing maintenance. Unlike solar PV (photovoltaic) systems that generate electricity, solar thermal systems primarily produce heat for various applications like water heating, space heating, or even power generation (Concentrated Solar Power - CSP).

Here's a comprehensive guide to the installation of a solar thermal plant:

1. Planning and Feasibility Study

   Before any physical installation begins, thorough planning is crucial.

* Assess Energy Needs: Determine the amount of hot water or heat required. This will dictate the size and type of solar thermal system needed. For example, a household will have different needs than a commercial or industrial application.
* Site Assessment:
* Location: Identify an area that receives ample, unobstructed direct sunlight throughout the day. For rooftop installations, assess the roof›s orientation (south-facing is generally ideal in the Northern Hemisphere) and pitch. For ground-mounted systems, consider land availability and proximity to the building where heat will be used.
* Shading Analysis: Identify and address any potential shading from trees, buildings, or other structures that could reduce system efficiency.
* Structural Integrity: For rooftop installations, ensure the roof can support the weight of the collectors and associated equipment.
* Proximity: The closer the collectors are to the storage tank and heat demand, the more efficient the system will be due to minimized heat loss in pipes.
* System Sizing: Based on energy needs and site assessment, calculate the appropriate size of the solar collectors and the hot water storage tank.

* Storage Tank: Typically, 15-20 gallons per person per day or per bedroom is a rough estimate for domestic hot water.
* Solar Collectors: Approximately 0.5 to 1 sq/ft of solar panels per gallon of storage is a general guideline.
* Choose Technology:
* Flat Plate Collectors: Common for residential and small commercial applications, good for moderate temperatures.
* Evacuated Tube Collectors: More efficient in colder climates or when higher temperatures are required.
* Concentrating Solar Power (CSP): Used for large-scale power generation, involving mirrors (parabolic troughs, power towers, dish/engine systems) to concentrate sunlight.
* Permits and Regulations: Research and obtain all necessary permits and approvals from local authorities, zoning boards, and building departments. This often includes environmental clearances, grid connectivity agreements (if applicable for CSP), and construction permits.
* Budget and Financing: Develop a detailed budget, including equipment, installation, and potential ongoing maintenance costs. Explore available subsidies, incentives, or financing options.
* Professional Consultation: Engage with authorized and experienced solar thermal installers or engineers. They can provide expert advice, conduct detailed assessments, and ensure compliance with standards.

2. Component Procurement

Acquire all necessary components based on the system design:

* Solar Collectors: Flat plate, evacuated tube, or concentrating collectors.
* Storage Tank: Insulated hot water storage tank, often specifically designed for solar thermal systems with multiple coils for heat exchange.
* Heat Exchanger: (If not integrated into the storage tank) Facilitates heat transfer from the collector›s fluid to the potable water or other heating medium.
* Piping: Insulated pipes suitable for high temperatures and the specific heat transfer fluid.
* Heat Transfer Fluid: Typically a glycol-water mixture for freeze protection in colder climates, or simply water in warmer regions.
* Circulation Pump: To circulate the heat transfer fluid between the collectors and the storage tank.
* Controller: A solar differential temperature controller that monitors temperatures in the collectors and the storage tank, activating the pump when heat can be collected.
* Expansion Tank: Accommodates the thermal expansion of the heat transfer fluid.
* Pressure Relief Valves and Air Vents: Safety devices to release excess pressure and purge air from the system.

* Mounting Hardware: Racks, brackets, and fasteners suitable for the roof or ground installation.
* Instrumentation: Temperature and pressure gauges, flow meters for monitoring.
* Auxiliary Heating System: Often integrated to provide heat when solar input is insufficient (e.g., a conventional water heater or boiler).

3. Installation Process

The installation sequence can vary slightly depending on the system type, but generally follows these steps:

* Site Preparation: Clear the installation area, ensure safe access (e.g., erect scaffolding for roof work), and protect the surrounding environment.
* Mounting Structure Installation:
* Roof-mounted: Secure mounting brackets and rails to the roof rafters, ensuring proper flashing and sealing of all roof penetrations to prevent leaks. The structure should be angled correctly to maximize solar exposure.
* Ground-mounted: Install a stable foundation and secure the mounting racks.
* Collector Installation: Carefully lift and secure the solar collectors onto the mounting structure. Ensure they are aligned correctly and firmly fastened.
* Piping and Plumbing:
* Primary Loop (Solar Circuit): Run insulated pipes from the collectors to the storage tank (or heat exchanger). Ensure proper sloping for drainage and air purging.
* Secondary Loop (Hot Water/Load Circuit): Connect the heat exchanger or storage tank to the building›s hot water system or other heating loads.
* Valves and Sensors: Install shut-off valves, check valves, pressure relief valves, air vents, and temperature/pressure sensors at appropriate points in the system.
* Storage Tank Installation: Position and secure the hot water storage tank, making necessary plumbing connections to the solar circuit and the building›s water supply.
* Pump and Controller Installation: Install the circulation pump(s) and the solar controller, wiring them according to manufacturer instructions. The controller will manage the pump operation based on temperature differentials.
* Electrical Wiring: For pumps, controllers, and any auxiliary heating elements, complete all necessary electrical wiring according to local codes. Ensure proper grounding.
* Integration with Auxiliary System: Connect the solar thermal system to any existing auxiliary heating system (e.g., boiler, electric water heater) to ensure a continuous supply of hot water or heat.

4. Commissioning

This critical phase ensures the system is operating correctly and safely.

* Flushing the Solar Circuit: Thoroughly flush the solar circuit to remove any debris, air, or impurities.
* Leak Testing: Pressurize the system and meticulously check all connections, pipes, and components for any leaks. Rectify any leaks immediately.
* Filling with Heat Transfer Fluid: Fill the solar circuit with the appropriate heat transfer fluid (e.g., glycol-water mixture) to the correct pressure.
* Setting Pump and Controller: Configure the pump and controller settings according to the system design and manufacturer specifications. This includes setting temperature differentials for pump activation.
* System Test and Operation:
* Start the system and monitor its operation.
* Verify that the pump is circulating fluid, the collectors are heating up, and heat is being transferred to the storage tank.
* Check temperatures at various points to ensure efficient heat collection.
* Confirm the proper functioning of all sensors, valves, and safety devices.
* Documentation and Handover: Provide the owner with all manuals, warranties, and a detailed explanation of system operation, maintenance requirements, and troubleshooting tips.

5. Maintenance and Monitoring

Regular maintenance is essential for optimal performance and longevity.

* Routine Checks: Periodically inspect collectors for dirt, dust, or damage. Clean collectors as needed.
* Fluid Levels and Quality: Check the heat transfer fluid level and condition. Top up or replace as necessary.
* Pump and Valve Inspection: Ensure pumps are operating smoothly and valves are functioning correctly.
* System Performance Monitoring: Monitor energy output, temperatures, and overall system efficiency. Many systems come with monitoring software or displays.
* Professional Servicing: Schedule periodic professional inspections and maintenance.

By following these steps, you can ensure a successful installation and efficient operation of a solar thermal plant. Always prioritize safety and consult with qualified professionals throughout the process.

Installing a solar thermal plant is a detailed process that involves several key stages, from initial planning to commissioning and ongoing maintenance. Unlike solar PV (photovoltaic) systems that generate electricity, solar thermal systems primarily produce heat for various applications like water heating, space heating, or even power generation (Concentrated Solar Power - CSP).

Here's a comprehensive guide to the installation of a solar thermal plant:

1. Planning and Feasibility Study
   Before any physical installation begins, thorough planning is crucial.

* Assess Energy Needs: Determine the amount of hot water or heat required. This will dictate the size and type of solar thermal system needed. For example, a household will have different needs than a commercial or industrial application.
* Site Assessment:
* Location: Identify an area that receives ample, unobstructed direct sunlight throughout the day. For rooftop installations, assess the roof›s orientation (south-facing is generally ideal in the Northern Hemisphere) and pitch. For ground-mounted systems, consider land availability and proximity to the building where heat will be used.
* Shading Analysis: Identify and address any potential shading from trees, buildings, or other structures that could reduce system efficiency.
* Structural Integrity: For rooftop installations, ensure the roof can support the weight of the collectors and associated equipment.
* Proximity: The closer the collectors are to the storage tank and heat demand, the more efficient the system will be due to minimized heat loss in pipes.
* System Sizing: Based on energy needs and site assessment, calculate the appropriate size of the solar collectors and the hot water storage tank.
* Storage Tank: Typically, 15-20 gallons per person per day or per bedroom is a rough estimate for domestic hot water.
* Solar Collectors: Approximately 0.5 to 1 sq/ft of solar panels per gallon of storage is a general guideline.
* Choose Technology:
* Flat Plate Collectors: Common for residential and small commercial applications, good for moderate temperatures.
* Evacuated Tube Collectors: More efficient in colder climates or when higher temperatures are required.
* Concentrating Solar Power (CSP): Used for large-scale power generation, involving mirrors (parabolic troughs, power towers, dish/engine systems) to concentrate sunlight.
* Permits and Regulations: Research and obtain all necessary permits and approvals from local authorities, zoning boards, and building departments. This often includes environmental clearances, grid connectivity agreements (if applicable for CSP), and construction permits.
* Budget and Financing: Develop a detailed budget, including equipment, installation, and potential ongoing maintenance costs. Explore available subsidies, incentives, or financing options.

* Professional Consultation: Engage with authorized and experienced solar thermal installers or engineers. They can provide expert advice, conduct detailed assessments, and ensure compliance with standards.

2. Component Procurement

Acquire all necessary components based on the system design:

* Solar Collectors: Flat plate, evacuated tube, or concentrating collectors.
* Storage Tank: Insulated hot water storage tank, often specifically designed for solar thermal systems with multiple coils for heat exchange.
* Heat Exchanger: (If not integrated into the storage tank) Facilitates heat transfer from the collector›s fluid to the potable water or other heating medium.
* Piping: Insulated pipes suitable for high temperatures and the specific heat transfer fluid.
* Heat Transfer Fluid: Typically a glycol-water mixture for freeze protection in colder climates, or simply water in warmer regions.
* Circulation Pump: To circulate the heat transfer fluid between the collectors and the storage tank.
* Controller: A solar differential temperature controller that monitors temperatures in the collectors and the storage tank, activating the pump when heat can be collected.
* Expansion Tank: Accommodates the thermal expansion of the heat transfer fluid.
* Pressure Relief Valves and Air Vents: Safety devices to release excess pressure and purge air from the system.
* Mounting Hardware: Racks, brackets, and fasteners suitable for the roof or ground installation.
* Instrumentation: Temperature and pressure gauges, flow meters for monitoring.
* Auxiliary Heating System: Often integrated to provide heat when solar input is insufficient (e.g., a conventional water heater or boiler).

3. Installation Process

The installation sequence can vary slightly depending on the system type, but generally follows these steps:

* Site Preparation: Clear the installation area, ensure safe access (e.g., erect scaffolding for roof work), and protect the surrounding environment.
* Mounting Structure Installation:
* Roof-mounted: Secure mounting brackets and rails to the roof rafters, ensuring proper flashing and sealing of all roof penetrations to prevent leaks. The structure should be angled correctly to maximize solar exposure.
* Ground-mounted: Install a stable foundation and secure the mounting racks.

* Collector Installation: Carefully lift and secure the solar collectors onto the mounting structure. Ensure they are aligned correctly and firmly fastened.
* Piping and Plumbing:
* Primary Loop (Solar Circuit): Run insulated pipes from the collectors to the storage tank (or heat exchanger). Ensure proper sloping for drainage and air purging.
* Secondary Loop (Hot Water/Load Circuit): Connect the heat exchanger or storage tank to the building›s hot water system or other heating loads.
* Valves and Sensors: Install shut-off valves, check valves, pressure relief valves, air vents, and temperature/pressure sensors at appropriate points in the system.
* Storage Tank Installation: Position and secure the hot water storage tank, making necessary plumbing connections to the solar circuit and the building›s water supply.
* Pump and Controller Installation: Install the circulation pump(s) and the solar controller, wiring them according to manufacturer instructions. The controller will manage the pump operation based on temperature differentials.
* Electrical Wiring: For pumps, controllers, and any auxiliary heating elements, complete all necessary electrical wiring according to local codes. Ensure proper grounding.
* Integration with Auxiliary System: Connect the solar thermal system to any existing auxiliary heating system (e.g., boiler, electric water heater) to ensure a continuous supply of hot water or heat.

4. Commissioning

This critical phase ensures the system is operating correctly and safely.

* Flushing the Solar Circuit: Thoroughly flush the solar circuit to remove any debris, air, or impurities.
* Leak Testing: Pressurize the system and meticulously check all connections, pipes, and components for any leaks. Rectify any leaks immediately.
* Filling with Heat Transfer Fluid: Fill the solar circuit with the appropriate heat transfer fluid (e.g., glycol-water mixture) to the correct pressure.
* Setting Pump and Controller: Configure the pump and controller settings according to the system design and manufacturer specifications. This includes setting temperature differentials for pump activation.
* System Test and Operation:
* Start the system and monitor its operation.
* Verify that the pump is circulating fluid, the collectors are heating up, and heat is being transferred to the storage tank.
* Check temperatures at various points to ensure efficient heat collection.

* Confirm the proper functioning of all sensors, valves, and safety devices.
* Documentation and Handover: Provide the owner with all manuals, warranties, and a detailed explanation of system operation, maintenance requirements, and troubleshooting tips.

5. Maintenance and Monitoring

   Regular maintenance is essential for optimal performance and longevity.

* Routine Checks: Periodically inspect collectors for dirt, dust, or damage. Clean collectors as needed.
* Fluid Levels and Quality: Check the heat transfer fluid level and condition. Top up or replace as necessary.
* Pump and Valve Inspection: Ensure pumps are operating smoothly and valves are functioning correctly.
* System Performance Monitoring: Monitor energy output, temperatures, and overall system efficiency. Many systems come with monitoring software or displays.
* Professional Servicing: Schedule periodic professional inspections and maintenance.

By following these steps, you can ensure a successful installation and efficient operation of a solar thermal plant. Always prioritize safety and consult with qualified professionals throughout the process.

Installing a solar thermal plant is a detailed process that involves several key stages, from initial planning to commissioning and ongoing maintenance. Unlike solar PV (photovoltaic) systems that generate electricity, solar thermal systems primarily produce heat for various applications like water heating, space heating, or even power generation (Concentrated Solar Power - CSP).

Here's a comprehensive guide to the installation of a solar thermal plant:

1. Planning and Feasibility Study

   Before any physical installation begins, thorough planning is crucial.

* Assess Energy Needs: Determine the amount of hot water or heat required. This will dictate the size and type of solar thermal system needed. For example, a household will have different needs than a commercial or industrial application.
* Site Assessment:
* Location: Identify an area that receives ample, unobstructed direct sunlight throughout the day. For rooftop installations, assess the roof's orientation (south-facing is generally ideal in the Northern Hemisphere) and pitch. For ground-mounted systems, consider land availability and proximity to the building where heat will be used.
* Shading Analysis: Identify and address any potential shading from trees, buildings, or other structures that could reduce system efficiency.

* Structural Integrity: For rooftop installations, ensure the roof can support the weight of the collectors and associated equipment.
* Proximity: The closer the collectors are to the storage tank and heat demand, the more efficient the system will be due to minimized heat loss in pipes.
* System Sizing: Based on energy needs and site assessment, calculate the appropriate size of the solar collectors and the hot water storage tank.
* Storage Tank: Typically, 15-20 gallons per person per day or per bedroom is a rough estimate for domestic hot water.
* Solar Collectors: Approximately 0.5 to 1 sq/ft of solar panels per gallon of storage is a general guideline.
* Choose Technology:
* Flat Plate Collectors: Common for residential and small commercial applications, good for moderate temperatures.
* Evacuated Tube Collectors: More efficient in colder climates or when higher temperatures are required.
* Concentrating Solar Power (CSP): Used for large-scale power generation, involving mirrors (parabolic troughs, power towers, dish/engine systems) to concentrate sunlight.
* Permits and Regulations: Research and obtain all necessary permits and approvals from local authorities, zoning boards, and building departments. This often includes environmental clearances, grid connectivity agreements (if applicable for CSP), and construction permits.
* Budget and Financing: Develop a detailed budget, including equipment, installation, and potential ongoing maintenance costs. Explore available subsidies, incentives, or financing options.
* Professional Consultation: Engage with authorized and experienced solar thermal installers or engineers. They can provide expert advice, conduct detailed assessments, and ensure compliance with standards.

2. Component Procurement

Acquire all necessary components based on the system design:

* Solar Collectors: Flat plate, evacuated tube, or concentrating collectors.
* Storage Tank: Insulated hot water storage tank, often specifically designed for solar thermal systems with multiple coils for heat exchange.
* Heat Exchanger: (If not integrated into the storage tank) Facilitates heat transfer from the collector›s fluid to the potable water or other heating medium.
* Piping: Insulated pipes suitable for high temperatures and the specific heat transfer fluid.
* Heat Transfer Fluid: Typically a glycol-water mixture for freeze protection in colder climates, or simply water in warmer regions.

* Circulation Pump: To circulate the heat transfer fluid between the collectors and the storage tank.
* Controller: A solar differential temperature controller that monitors temperatures in the collectors and the storage tank, activating the pump when heat can be collected.
* Expansion Tank: Accommodates the thermal expansion of the heat transfer fluid.
* Pressure Relief Valves and Air Vents: Safety devices to release excess pressure and purge air from the system.
* Mounting Hardware: Racks, brackets, and fasteners suitable for the roof or ground installation.
* Instrumentation: Temperature and pressure gauges, flow meters for monitoring.
* Auxiliary Heating System: Often integrated to provide heat when solar input is insufficient (e.g., a conventional water heater or boiler).

3. Installation Process

The installation sequence can vary slightly depending on the system type, but generally follows these steps:

* Site Preparation: Clear the installation area, ensure safe access (e.g., erect scaffolding for roof work), and protect the surrounding environment.
* Mounting Structure Installation:
* Roof-mounted: Secure mounting brackets and rails to the roof rafters, ensuring proper flashing and sealing of all roof penetrations to prevent leaks. The structure should be angled correctly to maximize solar exposure.
* Ground-mounted: Install a stable foundation and secure the mounting racks.
* Collector Installation: Carefully lift and secure the solar collectors onto the mounting structure. Ensure they are aligned correctly and firmly fastened.
* Piping and Plumbing:
* Primary Loop (Solar Circuit): Run insulated pipes from the collectors to the storage tank (or heat exchanger). Ensure proper sloping for drainage and air purging.
* Secondary Loop (Hot Water/Load Circuit): Connect the heat exchanger or storage tank to the building›s hot water system or other heating loads.
* Valves and Sensors: Install shut-off valves, check valves, pressure relief valves, air vents, and temperature/pressure sensors at appropriate points in the system.
* Storage Tank Installation: Position and secure the hot water storage tank, making necessary plumbing connections to the solar circuit and the building›s water supply.
* Pump and Controller Installation: Install the circulation pump(s) and the solar controller, wiring them according to manufacturer instructions. The controller will manage the pump operation based on temperature differentials.

* Electrical Wiring: For pumps, controllers, and any auxiliary heating elements, complete all necessary electrical wiring according to local codes. Ensure proper grounding.
* Integration with Auxiliary System: Connect the solar thermal system to any existing auxiliary heating system (e.g., boiler, electric water heater) to ensure a continuous supply of hot water or heat.

4. Commissioning
   This critical phase ensures the system is operating correctly and safely.
* Flushing the Solar Circuit: Thoroughly flush the solar circuit to remove any debris, air, or impurities.
* Leak Testing: Pressurize the system and meticulously check all connections, pipes, and components for any leaks. Rectify any leaks immediately.
* Filling with Heat Transfer Fluid: Fill the solar circuit with the appropriate heat transfer fluid (e.g., glycol-water mixture) to the correct pressure.
* Setting Pump and Controller: Configure the pump and controller settings according to the system design and manufacturer specifications. This includes setting temperature differentials for pump activation.
* System Test and Operation:
* Start the system and monitor its operation.
* Verify that the pump is circulating fluid, the collectors are heating up, and heat is being transferred to the storage tank.
* Check temperatures at various points to ensure efficient heat collection.
* Confirm the proper functioning of all sensors, valves, and safety devices.
* Documentation and Handover: Provide the owner with all manuals, warranties, and a detailed explanation of system operation, maintenance requirements, and troubleshooting tips.

5. Maintenance and Monitoring
   Regular maintenance is essential for optimal performance and longevity.
* Routine Checks: Periodically inspect collectors for dirt, dust, or damage. Clean collectors as needed.
* Fluid Levels and Quality: Check the heat transfer fluid level and condition. Top up or replace as necessary.
* Pump and Valve Inspection: Ensure pumps are operating smoothly and valves are functioning correctly.
* System Performance Monitoring: Monitor energy output, temperatures, and overall system efficiency. Many systems come with monitoring software or displays.
* Professional Servicing: Schedule periodic professional inspections and maintenance.

By following these steps, you can ensure a successful installation and efficient operation of a solar thermal plant. Always prioritize safety and consult with qualified professionals throughout the process.

A techno-economic analysis of solar thermal technology involves evaluating both its technical performance and its economic viability. This type of analysis is crucial for determining the feasibility and competitiveness of a solar thermal project, whether it's a small-scale residential water heater or a large-scale concentrating solar power (CSP) plant.

Here's a breakdown of the key elements of a techno-economic analysis for solar thermal technology:

1. Technical Performance Evaluation

   This part of the analysis focuses on how well the system works. Key metrics include:

* Solar Resource Assessment: The amount and quality of solar radiation available at a specific location are fundamental. This includes direct normal irradiance (DNI) for concentrating systems and global horizontal irradiance (GHI) for flat-plate collectors.
* System Efficiency: This measures how much of the incoming solar energy is converted into useful thermal energy or electricity. This is influenced by factors like collector design, operating temperature, and heat losses.
* Thermal Energy Output: The total amount of heat produced by the system, often measured in gigajoules (GJ) or kilowatt-hours thermal (kWhth).
* Electricity Generation (for CSP): For power plants, this includes the net electrical output, often measured in kilowatt-hours electrical (kWhe) or megawatt-hours electrical (MWh).
* System Sizing and Design: Optimizing the size of the collector field, storage system, and other components to meet a specific energy demand.
* Thermal Energy Storage (TES): Evaluating the capacity and efficiency of the storage system, which is crucial for providing dispatchable power or heat when the sun is not shining.
* Operational Parameters: Analyzing how factors like fluid flow rate, operating temperature, and cleaning schedules affect performance.

2. Economic Viability Assessment

   This part of the analysis focuses on the costs and revenues associated with the project. Key metrics include:

* Capital Expenditure (CAPEX): The initial investment required to build the system. This includes the cost of collectors, heat exchangers, pumps, piping, storage tanks, land, and installation.
* Operational Expenditure (OPEX): The ongoing costs of running the system. This includes maintenance, cleaning, labor, and water.

* Levelized Cost of Heat (LCOH) or Electricity (LCOE): This is a key metric that represents the average cost per unit of energy produced over the system›s lifetime. It›s a way to compare the cost of solar thermal with other energy sources. The formula is:

LCOE = \frac{\text{Sum of all costs over lifetime}}{\text{Sum of all energy produced over lifetime}} A lower LCOE or LCOH indicates a more economically viable project.

* Payback Period: The time it takes for the savings from using solar thermal energy to equal the initial investment. A shorter payback period is generally more attractive.
* Net Present Value (NPV): A financial metric that measures the profitability of a project by considering the time value of money. A positive NPV indicates that the project is expected to be profitable.
* Internal Rate of Return (IRR): The discount rate at which the NPV of all cash flows from a project equals zero. A higher IRR indicates a more profitable project.
* Sensitivity Analysis: This involves testing how changes in key variables (like solar irradiance, fuel prices, or interest rates) affect the economic outcomes. This helps to identify risks and opportunities.

Key Findings from Techno-Economic Analyses

Recent studies and analyses in the field of solar thermal technology often highlight the following points:

* High-Temperature Industrial Process Heat: There is a significant and growing interest in using solar thermal for industrial processes that require high temperatures. Techno-economic analyses are being used to optimize the design of these systems (e.g., concentrating solar thermal with thermal storage) to achieve the lowest possible LCOH.
* Hybrid Systems: The combination of solar thermal with other technologies, such as Photovoltaic-Thermal (PV-T) collectors or biomass, is a subject of research. These hybrid systems can produce both heat and electricity, and techno-economic analysis helps to determine their viability for different applications.
* Cost Reductions: Continued research and development are focused on reducing the cost of solar thermal components and improving their efficiency. This is a key factor in making solar thermal more competitive with traditional energy sources.
* Dispatchability: The ability of CSP plants with thermal energy storage to provide power on demand, even after sunset, is a major technical and economic advantage. Analyses show that this dispatchability can be highly valuable to the grid, especially in areas with high penetration of intermittent renewables like solar PV and wind.
* Location-Specific Analysis: The economic viability of solar thermal projects is highly dependent on the specific location's solar resource, local energy prices, and government policies (e.g.,

subsidies, carbon taxes). Therefore, a detailed, site-specific techno-economic analysis is essential for any pro

Climate Change Mitigation

Solar thermal energy plays a significant and distinct role in climate change mitigation by directly addressing the demand for heat and, in some cases, electricity, without relying on fossil fuels. Unlike solar photovoltaic (PV) technology which converts sunlight directly into electricity, solar thermal technology converts sunlight into heat.

Here's a breakdown of its key contributions to climate mitigation:

1. Decarbonizing Heat Demand
   A substantial portion of global energy consumption and associated greenhouse gas emissions comes from heating (for residential, commercial, and industrial purposes). Solar thermal energy directly addresses this by providing a clean, renewable source of heat.

* Residential and Commercial Hot Water and Space Heating: Solar thermal systems are widely used to heat water for domestic use, swimming pools, and to provide space heating in buildings. By replacing conventional boilers and water heaters that burn fossil fuels (natural gas, oil, coal) or rely on electricity generated from fossil fuels, solar thermal significantly reduces the associated CO_2 emissions.
* District Heating and Cooling: In urban areas, large-scale solar thermal plants can contribute to district heating networks, supplying heat to multiple buildings. This can lead to substantial reductions in fossil fuel consumption for an entire community. Solar thermal can also be used for solar cooling through absorption or adsorption chillers, further displacing electricity-intensive conventional cooling systems.
* Industrial Process Heat (SHIP - Solar Heat for Industrial Pr

Envernoment Impact

Solar thermal energy, which converts sunlight into heat, has a generally positive impact on the environment, primarily by displacing fossil fuel consumption. However, like all energy technologies, it also has some environmental considerations, particularly for large-scale Concentrated Solar Power (CSP) plants.

Here's a breakdown of the environmental effects:

Positive Environmental Effects

* Significant Reduction in Greenhouse Gas Emissions:

* Zero Operational Emissions: During operation, solar thermal systems do not burn fuel, thus producing virtually no greenhouse gases (CO_2, CH_4, N_2O) or other air pollutants (like sulfur dioxide (SO_2) and nitrogen oxides (NO_x)).
* Displacement of Fossil Fuels: By providing clean heat for residential, commercial, and industrial applications, and clean electricity via Concentrated Solar Power (CSP), solar thermal directly reduces the need for energy generated from fossil fuels. This is crucial for mitigating climate change and improving air quality.
* Lower Life-Cycle Emissions: While there are emissions associated with the manufacturing, transportation, and installation of solar thermal components, the overall life-cycle greenhouse gas emissions are significantly lower than those of fossil fuel-based energy systems. Solar thermal systems typically «pay back» the energy and emissions associated with their production within a few years and then operate cleanly for decades.
* Improved Air Quality:
* The reduction in fossil fuel combustion directly translates to less release of harmful air pollutants, leading to cleaner air and fewer respiratory and cardiovascular health issues for communities.
* Reduced Water Pollution:
* Unlike fossil fuel power plants that can discharge pollutants into water bodies, solar thermal systems, especially smaller-scale ones like solar water heaters, do not typically pollute water during operation.
* Conservation of Finite Resources:
* By relying on the inexhaustible energy of the sun, solar thermal technology reduces the consumption of finite fossil fuels, preserving these resources for future

Environmental Considerations and Potential Negative Effects

While the net environmental impact is positive, large-scale solar thermal (especially CSP) projects can have localized environmental considerations:

* Land Use and Habitat Loss:
* Large Footprint: Utility-scale CSP plants, like large solar PV farms, require significant land areas to collect enough sunlight. This can lead to concerns about land degradation, habitat fragmentation, and loss of biodiversity, especially if sited in ecologically sensitive areas. Estimates for CSP facilities can range from 4 to 16.5 acres per megawatt.
* Mitigation: Careful site selection (e.g., using brownfields, abandoned mining land, or non-agricultural areas) and effective land management practices (like establishing native groundcover) can help minimize these impacts.
* Water Consumption (Primarily for CSP with Wet Cooling):
* Cooling Systems: CSP plants that generate electricity often use water for cooling, similar to conventional thermal power plants. Wet-recirculating cooling systems, which rely on

evaporation, can consume substantial amounts of water. This is a significant concern in arid regions where solar resources are often abundant but water is scarce.

* Mirror Cleaning: Large arrays of mirrors in CSP plants require regular cleaning to maintain efficiency, which also consumes water, especially in dusty, dry environments.
* Mitigation: Technologies like dry-cooling or hybrid wet/dry cooling systems can significantly reduce water consumption (by 75-95%). Research and development are ongoing to further minimize water use in CSP plants, including optimizing mirror cleaning strategies and implementing comprehensive water management plans. Smaller-scale solar thermal systems (like solar water heaters) generally have minimal operational water requirements.
* Use of Hazardous Materials:
* Manufacturing: The manufacturing of solar thermal components, like any industrial process, involves the use of various materials, some of which can be hazardous (e.g., certain metals or heat transfer fluids). Proper handling and disposal are crucial to prevent environmental release.
* Heat Transfer Fluids (CSP): Some CSP systems use specialized fluids (e.g., synthetic oils or molten salts) to transfer heat. While generally contained, leaks of these materials could pose localized environmental risks if not properly managed.
* End-of-Life Disposal: As solar thermal systems reach the end of their operational life (typically 20-30 years), proper recycling and disposal of components are essential to prevent hazardous materials from entering the environment and to recover valuable resources.
* Visual Impact and Noise:
* Large solar thermal installations can have a visual impact on the landscape, which can be a concern for local communities.
* While generally quieter than fossil fuel plants, some components (like pumps or turbines in CSP) can generate noise.

In conclusion, solar thermal energy offers substantial environmental benefits, particularly in reducing greenhouse gas emissions and air pollution by displacing fossil fuels. The main environmental challenges are associated with large-scale CSP plants, primarily concerning land use and water consumption (especially in arid regions). Ongoing technological advancements and careful project planning are continuously working to mitigate these potential negative impacts, making solar thermal an increasingly sustainable and crucial part of the clean energy transition.

Climate Change Mitigation

Solar thermal energy plays a significant and distinct role in climate change mitigation by directly addressing the demand for heat and, in some cases, electricity, without relying on fossil fuels. Unlike solar photovoltaic (PV) technology which converts sunlight directly into electricity, solar thermal technology converts sunlight into heat.

Here's a breakdown of its key contributions to climate mitigation:

1. Decarbonizing Heat Demand
   A substantial portion of global energy consumption and associated greenhouse gas emissions comes from heating (for residential, commercial, and industrial purposes). Solar thermal energy directly addresses this by providing a clean, renewable source of heat.

* Residential and Commercial Hot Water and Space Heating: Solar thermal systems are widely used to heat water for domestic use, swimming pools, and to provide space heating in buildings. By replacing conventional boilers and water heaters that burn fossil fuels (natural gas, oil, coal) or rely on electricity generated from fossil fuels, solar thermal significantly reduces the associated CO_2 emissions.
* District Heating and Cooling: In urban areas, large-scale solar thermal plants can contribute to district heating networks, supplying heat to multiple buildings. This can lead to substantial reductions in fossil fuel consumption for an entire community. Solar thermal can also be used for solar cooling through absorption or adsorption chillers, further displacing electricity-intensive conventional cooling systems.
* Industrial Process Heat (SHIP - Solar Heat for Industrial Pr

Solar thermal energy plays a significant and distinct role in climate change mitigation by directly addressing the demand for heat and, in some cases, electricity, without relying on fossil fuels. Unlike solar photovoltaic (PV) technology which converts sunlight directly into electricity, solar thermal technology converts sunlight into heat.

Here's a breakdown of its key contributions to climate mitigation:

1. Decarbonizing Heat Demand
   A substantial portion of global energy consumption and associated greenhouse gas emissions comes from heating (for residential, commercial, and industrial purposes). Solar thermal energy directly addresses this by providing a clean, renewable source of heat.

* Residential and Commercial Hot Water and Space Heating: Solar thermal systems are widely used to heat water for domestic use, swimming pools, and to provide space heating in buildings. By replacing conventional boilers and water heaters that burn fossil fuels (natural gas, oil, coal) or rely on electricity generated from fossil fuels, solar thermal significantly reduces the associated CO_2 emissions.
* District Heating and Cooling: In urban areas, large-scale solar thermal plants can contribute to district heating networks, supplying heat to multiple buildings. This can lead to substantial reductions in fossil fuel consumption for an entire community. Solar thermal can also be used for solar cooling through absorption or adsorption chillers, further displacing electricity-intensive conventional cooling systems.

Solar thermal energy plays a significant and distinct role in climate change mitigation by directly addressing the demand for heat and, in some cases, electricity, without relying on fossil fuels. Unlike solar photovoltaic (PV) technology which converts sunlight directly into electricity, solar thermal technology converts sunlight into heat.

Here's a breakdown of its key contributions to climate mitigation:

1. Decarbonizing Heat Demand
   A substantial portion of global energy consumption and associated greenhouse gas emissions comes from heating (for residential, commercial, and industrial purposes). Solar thermal energy directly addresses this by providing a clean, renewable source of heat.

* Residential and Commercial Hot Water and Space Heating: Solar thermal systems are widely used to heat water for domestic use, swimming pools, and to provide space heating in buildings. By replacing conventional boilers and water heaters that burn fossil fuels (natural gas, oil, coal) or rely on electricity generated from fossil fuels, solar thermal significantly reduces the associated CO_2 emissions.
* District Heating and Cooling: In urban areas, large-scale solar thermal plants can contribute to district heating networks, supplying heat to multiple buildings. This can lead to substantial reductions in fossil fuel consumption for an entire community. Solar thermal can also be used for solar cooling through absorption or adsorption chillers, further displacing electricity-intensive conventional cooling systems.
* Industrial Process Heat (SHIP - Solar Heat for Industrial Processes): Man

Solar thermal energy plays a significant and distinct role in climate change mitigation by directly addressing the demand for heat and, in some cases, electricity, without relying on fossil fuels. Unlike solar photovoltaic (PV) technology which converts sunlight directly into electricity, solar thermal technology converts sunlight into heat.

Here's a breakdown of its key contributions to climate mitigation:

1. Decarbonizing Heat Demand
   A substantial portion of global energy consumption and associated greenhouse gas emissions comes from heating (for residential, commercial, and industrial purposes). Solar thermal energy directly addresses this by providing a clean, renewable source of heat.

* Residential and Commercial Hot Water and Space Heating: Solar thermal systems are widely used to heat water for domestic use, swimming pools, and to provide space heating in buildings. By replacing conventional boilers and water heaters that burn fossil fuels (natural gas, oil, coal) or rely on electricity generated from fossil fuels, solar thermal significantly reduces the associated CO_2 emissions.

* District Heating and Cooling: In urban areas, large-scale solar thermal plants can contribute to district heating networks, supplying heat to multiple buildings. This can lead to substantial reductions in fossil fuel consumption for an entire community. Solar thermal can also be used for solar cooling through absorption or adsorption chillers, further displacing electricity-intensive conventional cooling systems.
* Industrial Process Heat (SHIP - Solar Heat for Industrial Processes): Many industries require heat for various processes like drying, cleaning, sterilization, pasteurization, and chemical reactions. Solar thermal technology can provide low to medium-temperature process heat, offering a sustainable and cost-effective alternative to fossil fuels in industrial settings. This is a crucial area for decarbonization as industrial heat demand is a major source of emissions.

2. Concentrated Solar Power (CSP) for Electricity Generation

While solar thermal primarily focuses on heat, a specific application, Concentrated Solar Power (CSP), uses solar thermal principles to generate electricity on a utility scale.

* Clean Electricity Production: CSP plants use mirrors (e.g., parabolic troughs, power towers, Fresnel reflectors, dish/engine systems) to concentrate sunlight onto a receiver, heating a fluid to very high temperatures. This heat then drives a turbine to generate electricity, similar to conventional thermal power plants, but without the emissions from burning fossil fuels.
* Dispatchable Power with Thermal Storage: A key advantage of CSP over solar PV is its inherent ability to integrate thermal energy storage (TES). The heat collected during sunny hours can be stored (e.g., in molten salt) and then used to generate electricity even after the sun sets or during cloudy periods. This «dispatchable» nature of CSP makes it a valuable asset for grid stability, allowing it to provide power on demand and reduce the need for fossil fuel backup plants. This capability significantly enhances the overall contribution of solar energy to a reliable, low-carbon grid.

3. Energy Independence and Efficiency

* Reduced Reliance on Fossil Fuels: By providing direct heat or electricity from sunlight, solar thermal technologies reduce dependence on finite and often imported fossil fuels, enhancing energy security for nations and individual users.
* Improved Energy Efficiency: Solar thermal systems can improve overall energy efficiency by utilizing a direct source of heat, minimizing conversion losses that might occur when converting fuel to electricity and then electricity back to heat.

In essence, solar thermal energy directly tackles the significant portion of global emissions stemming from heating demands and provides a dispatchable, clean electricity option through CSP. Its ability to replace fossil fuels in these critical sectors makes it an indispensable technology for comprehensive climate change mitigation efforts.

Solar thermal energy plays a significant and distinct role in climate change mitigation by directly addressing the demand for heat and, in some cases, electricity, without relying on fossil fuels. Unlike solar photovoltaic (PV) technology which converts sunlight directly into electricity, solar thermal technology converts sunlight into heat.

Here's a breakdown of its key contributions to climate mitigation:

1. Decarbonizing Heat Demand

   A substantial portion of global energy consumption and associated greenhouse gas emissions comes from heating (for residential, commercial, and industrial purposes). Solar thermal energy directly addresses this by providing a clean, renewable source of heat.

* Residential and Commercial Hot Water and Space Heating: Solar thermal systems are widely used to heat water for domestic use, swimming pools, and to provide space heating in buildings. By replacing conventional boilers and water heaters that burn fossil fuels (natural gas, oil, coal) or rely on electricity generated from fossil fuels, solar thermal significantly reduces the associated CO_2 emissions.
* District Heating and Cooling: In urban areas, large-scale solar thermal plants can contribute to district heating networks, supplying heat to multiple buildings. This can lead to substantial reductions in fossil fuel consumption for an entire community. Solar thermal can also be used for solar cooling through absorption or adsorption chillers, further displacing electricity-intensive conventional cooling systems.
* Industrial Process Heat (SHIP - Solar Heat for Industrial Processes): Many industries require heat for various processes like drying, cleaning, sterilization, pasteurization, and chemical reactions. Solar thermal technology can provide low to medium-temperature process heat, offering a sustainable and cost-effective alternative to fossil fuels in industrial settings. This is a crucial area for decarbonization as industrial heat demand is a major source of emissions.

2. Concentrated Solar Power (CSP) for Electricity Generation

   While solar thermal primarily focuses on heat, a specific application, Concentrated Solar Power (CSP), uses solar thermal principles to generate electricity on a utility scale.

* Clean Electricity Production: CSP plants use mirrors (e.g., parabolic troughs, power towers, Fresnel reflectors, dish/engine systems) to concentrate sunlight onto a receiver, heating a fluid to very high temperatures. This heat then drives a turbine to generate electricity, similar to conventional thermal power plants, but without the emissions from burning fossil fuels.
* Dispatchable Power with Thermal Storage: A key advantage of CSP over solar PV is its inherent ability to integrate thermal energy storage (TES). The heat collected during sunny hours can be stored (e.g., in molten salt) and then used to generate electricity even after the sun sets or during cloudy periods. This «dispatchable» nature of CSP makes it a valuable asset for grid stability, allowing it to provide power on demand and reduce the need for fossil fuel

backup plants. This capability significantly enhances the overall contribution of solar energy to a reliable, low-carbon grid.

3. Energy Independence and Efficiency

* Reduced Reliance on Fossil Fuels: By providing direct heat or electricity from sunlight, solar thermal technologies reduce dependence on finite and often imported fossil fuels, enhancing energy security for nations and individual users.
* Improved Energy Efficiency: Solar thermal systems can improve overall energy efficiency by utilizing a direct source of heat, minimizing conversion losses that might occur when converting fuel to electricity and then electricity back to heat.

In essence, solar thermal energy directly tackles the significant portion of global emissions stemming from heating demands and provides a dispatchable, clean electricity option through CSP. Its ability to replace fossil fuels in these critical sectors makes it an indispensable technology for comprehensive climate change mitigation efforts.

Use Of Computer Modeling

Computer modeling plays an absolutely critical role in the planning, design, optimization, and evaluation of solar thermal devices and systems. It allows engineers and designers to simulate complex thermal processes, predict performance under various conditions, and make informed decisions without the need for costly and time-consuming physical prototypes.

Here's how computer modeling is used in the planning of solar thermal devices:

1. Performance Prediction and Sizing

* Simulating Energy Collection: Models can accurately predict how much solar radiation a collector will absorb based on its design, orientation, tilt angle, and the specific geographic location›s climate data (e.g., hourly solar irradiance, ambient temperature, wind speed).
* Thermal Performance Analysis: They simulate the heat transfer within the collector and the entire system (e.g., heat exchangers, storage tanks, pipes). This includes calculating heat losses due to conduction, convection, and radiation, and determining the useful heat gained.
* System Sizing: Based on the predicted heat demand (for hot water, space heating, or industrial processes) and the solar resource, models help determine the optimal size and number of solar collectors, as well as the appropriate volume for thermal storage tanks. This ensures the system is neither undersized (leading to insufficient energy) nor oversized (leading to unnecessary costs).
* Dynamic Simulation: Advanced software can perform dynamic annual simulations, calculating temperatures and energy flows in very small time increments (e.g., every 6 minutes) over an

entire year. This provides a highly accurate picture of system performance under fluctuating real-world conditions.

2. Design Optimization

* Collector Design: Computer models, including Computational Fluid Dynamics (CFD) and ray tracing, are used to optimize the geometry and materials of solar collectors (e.g., absorber plate design, glazing properties, vacuum levels in evacuated tubes) to maximize heat absorption and minimize heat loss.
* System Configuration: They help optimize the arrangement of collectors (series-parallel arrays), the sizing of pumps, and the control strategies (e.g., optimal flow rates, switching temperatures for pumps) to achieve the highest efficiency and cost-effectiveness.
* Integration with Other Systems: Models can simulate the integration of solar thermal systems with auxiliary heating sources (like boilers), heat pumps, or even other renewable energy technologies (like solar PV in hybrid systems) to ensure seamless operation and maximize overall energy savings.
* Thermal Energy Storage Optimization: Models are crucial for designing and optimizing thermal energy storage systems, determining the ideal storage medium (e.g., water, molten salt, phase-change materials), tank size, and insulation to meet demand profiles.

3. Economic and Environmental Assessment

* Cost-Benefit Analysis: Models can integrate economic parameters (e.g., initial investment costs, operational costs, energy prices, government incentives, subsidies) to perform profitability analyses, calculate payback periods, and determine the life cycle savings of a solar thermal system.
* Environmental Impact Assessment: By predicting the amount of fossil fuel displaced, models can quantify the reduction in greenhouse gas emissions and other pollutants, providing a clear environmental benefit assessment.
* Variant Comparison: Many software tools allow for the comparison of multiple design variants side-by-side, evaluating their performance, costs, and environmental impacts to help select the most suitable solution.

4. Site-Specific Analysis

* Climate Data Integration: Models utilize extensive databases of climate data (e.g., Meteonorm) for specific geographic locations worldwide, allowing for highly accurate, site-specific performance predictions. Users can also import their own measured climate data.

* Shading Analysis: Advanced tools can perform detailed 2D or 3D shading analysis, considering surrounding buildings, trees, and other obstructions, to ensure optimal placement and orientation of solar collectors and minimize performance losses due to shading.

Common Computer Modeling Tools and Techniques

* TRNSYS (Transient System Simulation Tool): A widely used modular simulation software for the dynamic simulation of energy systems, including solar thermal installations. It›s known for its high accuracy but requires considerable training.
* T*SOL: Specialized software for designing and simulating solar thermal systems, offering detailed performance predictions, economic analyses, and customizable reports.
* MATLAB/Simulink: Used for developing custom mathematical models and simulations of solar thermal components and systems, allowing for in-depth analysis and optimization.
* Computational Fluid Dynamics (CFD): Software like SimScale (cloud-based) or ANSYS Fluent is used for detailed analysis of fluid flow and heat transfer within collectors and other components, optimizing their internal design.
* Spreadsheet-based tools: For simpler analyses, custom tools built in spreadsheets can perform parametric analyses and basic performance calculations.

By leveraging these computer modeling capabilities, engineers and designers can plan and deploy solar thermal devices that are highly efficient, cost-effective, and optimally suited for their specific applications, accelerating the transition to a sustainable energy future.

Remote Sencing

Remote sensing plays a crucial and growing role in the planning, design, and operation of solar thermal devices and systems. By using data collected from satellites, aircraft, and drones, planners can make informed decisions that optimize performance, reduce costs, and minimize environmental impact.

Here are the key uses of remote sensing in solar thermal energy:

1. Solar Resource Assessment

   This is is the most fundamental application. Solar thermal systems, especially Concentrated Solar Power (CSP) plants, require accurate and reliable data on the amount and type of solar radiation available at a given site.

* Irradiance Mapping: Remote sensing satellites measure solar radiation reaching the Earth›s surface. This data is used to create highly detailed maps of Direct Normal Irradiance (DNI) and Global Horizontal Irradiance (GHI). DNI is particularly critical for CSP, which requires direct, concentrated sunlight, while GHI is more relevant for smaller-scale systems like solar water heaters.

* Atmospheric Analysis: Remote sensing helps monitor atmospheric conditions like cloud cover, aerosols (dust, smoke), and water vapor, which can significantly attenuate solar radiation. This data allows for more accurate long-term solar resource models and short-term forecasting.
* Long-Term Data: Satellite-based data provides consistent, long-term records of solar radiation, enabling planners to analyze historical trends and seasonal variations, which is essential for accurate energy yield predictions and financial modeling.

2. Site Suitability Analysis and Selection

Remote sensing, often integrated with Geographic Information Systems (GIS), allows for a comprehensive analysis of potential sites, which is vital for large-scale solar thermal projects.

* Land Use and Land Cover Mapping: High-resolution satellite imagery helps identify suitable land areas, such as degraded land, barren land, or arid regions that are not used for agriculture. It helps avoid ecologically sensitive areas and minimizes the environmental footprint of large-scale projects.
* Topography and Terrain Analysis: Using data from remote sensing technologies like LiDAR, planners can create detailed Digital Elevation Models (DEMs). This allows for the analysis of terrain slope, orientation (aspect), and elevation, which are crucial for optimizing collector tilt angles and avoiding self-shading, ensuring the maximum amount of sunlight is captured throughout the day and year.
* Shading Analysis: By analyzing satellite and aerial imagery, remote sensing helps model and predict shading from surrounding geographical features (e.g., hills, mountains) or man-made structures (e.g., tall buildings). This is critical for both large CSP farms and urban rooftop installations.
* Proximity to Infrastructure: Satellite imagery helps planners assess a site›s proximity to existing infrastructure like roads for access and transmission lines/substations for grid connection. This is a key factor in the economic feasibility of CSP plants.

3. Urban Planning and Rooftop Potential

For urban areas where distributed solar thermal systems (like solar water heaters) are more common, remote sensing offers a powerful planning tool.

* Rooftop Potential Mapping: High-resolution satellite imagery can be used to automatically identify suitable rooftops for solar thermal collectors. Algorithms can analyze the size, shape, and orientation of roofs and their exposure to sunlight, creating detailed maps of urban solar potential. This allows city planners to streamline permitting processes and incentivize adoption in the most suitable locations.
* Urban Heat Island Mitigation: Thermal remote sensing (using infrared data) can help identify areas with high urban heat island effect, where solar thermal systems could be installed to both provide hot water and potentially help reduce surface temperatures.

4. Performance Monitoring and Maintenance
   Remote sensing can be used to monitor operational solar thermal systems, improving efficiency and reducing maintenance costs.

* Mirror and Collector Soiling: In large-scale CSP plants, dust and dirt accumulation on mirrors (soiling) can significantly reduce efficiency. Remote sensing (e.g., using drones with high-resolution cameras) can identify areas with heavy soiling, helping to optimize cleaning schedules and conserve water.
* Fault Detection: Thermal remote sensing can detect «hot spots» in solar thermal components that may indicate a fault or defect, allowing for early intervention and repair before a major failure occurs.
* Operational Validation: Satellite data on solar irradiance can be used to validate the actual energy output of a solar thermal plant against its predicted performance, helping operators identify and address any discrepancies.

Envernoment Impact

Solar thermal energy, which converts sunlight into heat, has a generally positive impact on the environment, primarily by displacing fossil fuel consumption. However, like all energy technologies, it also has some environmental considerations, particularly for large-scale Concentrated Solar Power (CSP) plants.

Here's a breakdown of the environmental effects:

Positive Environmental Effects

* Significant Reduction in Greenhouse Gas Emissions:
* Zero Operational Emissions: During operation, solar thermal systems do not burn fuel, thus producing virtually no greenhouse gases (CO_2, CH_4, N_2O) or other air pollutants (like sulfur dioxide (SO_2) and nitrogen oxides (NO_x)).
* Displacement of Fossil Fuels: By providing clean heat for residential, commercial, and industrial applications, and clean electricity via Concentrated Solar Power (CSP), solar thermal directly reduces the need for energy generated from fossil fuels. This is crucial for mitigating climate change and improving air quality.
* Lower Life-Cycle Emissions: While there are emissions associated with the manufacturing, transportation, and installation of solar thermal components, the overall life-cycle greenhouse gas emissions are significantly lower than those of fossil fuel-based energy systems. Solar thermal systems typically «pay back» the energy and emissions associated with their production within a few years and then operate cleanly for decades.
* Improved Air Quality:

* The reduction in fossil fuel combustion directly translates to less release of harmful air pollutants, leading to cleaner air and fewer respiratory and cardiovascular health issues for communities.
* Reduced Water Pollution:
* Unlike fossil fuel power plants that can discharge pollutants into water bodies, solar thermal systems, especially smaller-scale ones like solar water heaters, do not typically pollute water during operation.
* Conservation of Finite Resources:
* By relying on the inexhaustible energy of the sun, solar thermal technology reduces the consumption of finite fossil fuels, preserving these resources for future

Environmental Considerations and Potential Negative Effects

While the net environmental impact is positive, large-scale solar thermal (especially CSP) projects can have localized environmental considerations:

* Land Use and Habitat Loss:
* Large Footprint: Utility-scale CSP plants, like large solar PV farms, require significant land areas to collect enough sunlight. This can lead to concerns about land degradation, habitat fragmentation, and loss of biodiversity, especially if sited in ecologically sensitive areas. Estimates for CSP facilities can range from 4 to 16.5 acres per megawatt.
* Mitigation: Careful site selection (e.g., using brownfields, abandoned mining land, or non-agricultural areas) and effective land management practices (like establishing native groundcover) can help minimize these impacts.
* Water Consumption (Primarily for CSP with Wet Cooling):
* Cooling Systems: CSP plants that generate electricity often use water for cooling, similar to conventional thermal power plants. Wet-recirculating cooling systems, which rely on evaporation, can consume substantial amounts of water. This is a significant concern in arid regions where solar resources are often abundant but water is scarce.
* Mirror Cleaning: Large arrays of mirrors in CSP plants require regular cleaning to maintain efficiency, which also consumes water, especially in dusty, dry environments.
* Mitigation: Technologies like dry-cooling or hybrid wet/dry cooling systems can significantly reduce water consumption (by 75-95%). Research and development are ongoing to further minimize water use in CSP plants, including optimizing mirror cleaning strategies and implementing comprehensive water management plans. Smaller-scale solar thermal systems (like solar water heaters) generally have minimal operational water requirements.
* Use of Hazardous Materials:
* Manufacturing: The manufacturing of solar thermal components, like any industrial process, involves the use of various materials, some of which can be hazardous (e.g., certain metals or heat transfer fluids). Proper handling and disposal are crucial to prevent environmental release.

* Heat Transfer Fluids (CSP): Some CSP systems use specialized fluids (e.g., synthetic oils or molten salts) to transfer heat. While generally contained, leaks of these materials could pose localized environmental risks if not properly managed.
* End-of-Life Disposal: As solar thermal systems reach the end of their operational life (typically 20-30 years), proper recycling and disposal of components are essential to prevent hazardous materials from entering the environment and to recover valuable resources.
* Visual Impact and Noise:
* Large solar thermal installations can have a visual impact on the landscape, which can be a concern for local communities.
* While generally quieter than fossil fuel plants, some components (like pumps or turbines in CSP) can generate noise.

In conclusion, solar thermal energy offers substantial environmental benefits, particularly in reducing greenhouse gas emissions and air pollution by displacing fossil fuels. The main environmental challenges are associated with large-scale CSP plants, primarily concerning land use and water consumption (especially in arid regions). Ongoing technological advancements and careful project planning are continuously working to mitigate these potential negative impacts, making solar thermal an increasingly sustainable and crucial part of the clean energy transition.

Climate Change Mitigation

Solar thermal energy plays a significant and distinct role in climate change mitigation by directly addressing the demand for heat and, in some cases, electricity, without relying on fossil fuels. Unlike solar photovoltaic (PV) technology which converts sunlight directly into electricity, solar thermal technology converts sunlight into heat.

Here's a breakdown of its key contributions to climate mitigation:

1. Decarbonizing Heat Demand
   A substantial portion of global energy consumption and associated greenhouse gas emissions comes from heating (for residential, commercial, and industrial purposes). Solar thermal energy directly addresses this by providing a clean, renewable source of heat.

* Residential and Commercial Hot Water and Space Heating: Solar thermal systems are widely used to heat water for domestic use, swimming pools, and to provide space heating in buildings. By replacing conventional boilers and water heaters that burn fossil fuels (natural gas, oil, coal) or rely on electricity generated from fossil fuels, solar thermal significantly reduces the associated CO_2 emissions.
* District Heating and Cooling: In urban areas, large-scale solar thermal plants can contribute to district heating networks, supplying heat to multiple buildings. This can lead to substantial reductions in fossil fuel consumption for an entire community. Solar thermal can also be

used for solar cooling through absorption or adsorption chillers, further displacing electricity-intensive conventional cooling systems.

* Industrial Process Heat (SHIP - Solar Heat for Industrial Pr

While "solar" energy is making significant strides in India's national energy mix, it's crucial to differentiate between Solar Photovoltaic (PV) and Solar Thermal (Concentrated Solar Power - CSP) when discussing their "share."

Solar PV (electricity generation) dominates the "solar" share in India:

* Massive Growth: India has seen an exponential increase in solar PV installed capacity. As of June 2025, India›s total installed solar PV capacity reached 116.247 GW, contributing a substantial 23.98% to India›s entire power mix, and representing 62.97% of the total renewable energy capacity. This is a remarkable achievement, making solar PV a cornerstone of India›s clean energy transition.
* Overall Energy Mix: While solar PV is growing rapidly, thermal power (primarily coal) still accounts for a dominant share of India›s electricity generation. As of April 2025, coal accounts for 45.02% of the total installed power capacity, and in 2024, coal generation met 64% of India›s electricity demand growth. Despite the increase in clean energy capacity, the actual electricity generated from these sources is still below 30% due to the Capacity Utilization Factor (CUF) of intermittent renewables like solar and wind.

Solar Thermal (CSP for electricity, and thermal applications) has a much smaller share in electricity generation, but plays a role in heating:

* Limited Utility-Scale CSP: India has a few utility-scale Concentrated Solar Power (CSP) plants, but their installed capacity is comparatively small compared to solar PV or conventional thermal plants. As of recent data, India has some operational CSP plants, but the cumulative installed capacity for solar thermal power generation is in the hundreds of megawatts, not gigawatts. For example, some reports mention a cumulative installed capacity of 232.5 MW for solar thermal power as of 2022, with a slow growth forecast.
* Focus on Process Heat: Where solar thermal truly contributes significantly is in direct heat applications, rather than large-scale electricity generation. These applications include:
* Solar Water Heaters: Widely used in residential, commercial (hotels, hospitals), and industrial sectors for hot water. India has an estimated installed capacity of around 6.8 million square meters of solar water heating systems.
* Industrial Process Heat: Solar thermal systems are increasingly being adopted by industries like food processing, textiles, chemicals, dairy, paper and pulp, etc., to provide heat for various processes. This helps in decarbonizing industrial operations.
* Solar Cooking: Smaller-scale solar thermal systems are also used for cooking.

* Space Heating/Cooling: Though less prevalent, some applications for space heating/cooling also exist.

Reasons for the difference:
* Cost-Effectiveness: Solar PV technology has seen dramatic cost reductions, making it highly competitive for electricity generation. CSP, particularly utility-scale power plants, often has higher capital costs and can be more complex to operate.
* Simplicity and Scalability: Solar PV panels are modular, easier to install, and can be scaled from rooftop systems to large solar farms.
* Land Requirements: Large-scale CSP plants with mirror fields require significant land area with high direct normal irradiance (DNI), which can be a limiting factor.

National Targets and Future Outlook:

India has an ambitious target of achieving 500 GW of non-fossil fuel capacity by 2030. While solar PV will contribute the lion's share of this, there's also a recognition of the potential of solar thermal for industrial process heat and other applications. Efforts are being made to promote Concentrated Solar Thermal (CST) for heat generation in industries, with a reported industrial market potential of around 6.45 GWth.

In conclusion, on a national scenario, solar PV holds a very prominent and rapidly growing share in India's electricity generation mix. Solar thermal for power generation (CSP) has a much smaller installed base, but solar thermal technology for direct heat applications (like water heating and industrial process heat) is a significant and growing area of contribution to India's overall energy landscape, playing a crucial role in decarbonizing specific sectors.

Contriution to GDP

The contribution of solar thermal technology to India's GDP

GDP is a complex issue, as it's not a single, easily quantifiable figure like that of the IT sector. Instead, its economic impact is multi-faceted and spread across various sectors. The contribution comes from several key areas:

1. Direct Economic Contribution
   This includes the direct market value of solar thermal products and services. While data for this is often fragmented, it provides a picture of the industry's size:
* Manufacturing and Installation: The solar thermal industry involves the manufacturing of components like solar collectors, storage tanks, and control systems. The market for solar water heaters alone in India is a significant business, with a market size projected to grow from around $351 million in FY2024 to over $613 million by FY2032.

* Large-Scale Projects (CSP): The development and construction of Concentrating Solar Power (CSP) plants contribute to GDP through capital expenditure, which includes the cost of land, equipment, and labor. While utility-scale CSP deployment has been slower in India compared to solar PV, there is still a market for these projects, particularly in hybrid systems.

2. Indirect Economic Contribution

This is where the impact of solar thermal technology becomes more widespread and harder to quantify precisely.

* Energy Cost Savings: Solar thermal systems, especially for water and space heating, help households and industries save on energy bills. These savings, which would have otherwise been spent on fossil fuels or electricity, can be redirected towards other economic activities, stimulating growth. For example, a report indicates that industrial units in India consume energy worth approximately $45 billion per year, and solar thermal can significantly reduce a portion of this cost.
* Reduced Import Bill: By reducing the need for fossil fuels, particularly for heating applications, solar thermal technology helps India lower its energy import bill. This reduces the country›s trade deficit and strengthens its economy. India still relies heavily on imported fossil fuels, so every unit of energy generated domestically from renewable sources is a net gain for the economy.
* Job Creation: The solar thermal sector, like the broader solar industry, creates jobs throughout its value chain. This includes roles in manufacturing, sales, installation, operation, and maintenance. While data specific to solar thermal jobs is limited, the overall solar sector in India is a significant source of employment.
* Industrial Productivity and Competitiveness: Industries that adopt solar thermal for process heat can become more competitive by lowering their operating costs and reducing their carbon footprint. This is a crucial factor for industries facing pressure to decarbonize. The use of Concentrating Solar Thermal (CST) for industrial heat has a market potential of around 6.45 GWth in India, which represents a massive opportunity for economic growth and carbon reduction.
* Promoting «Make in India» and Local Manufacturing: The growth of the solar thermal industry encourages domestic manufacturing of components, reducing reliance on imports and supporting the «Make in India» initiative. This boosts local industries and helps create a self-reliant economy.

3. Challenges and Future Potential

While the contribution of solar thermal is currently a small fraction of India's overall GDP compared to solar PV, its potential is substantial.

* Policy Support: The government›s focus has been largely on solar PV for electricity generation. However, there is a growing recognition of the role of solar thermal in addressing the heating and cooling needs of buildings and industries. Specific policies and incentives for solar thermal could unlock significant economic potential.
* Technological Advancement: Continued research and development, particularly in Concentrating Solar-Thermal (CST) technologies and thermal energy storage, will be crucial for increasing efficiency and reducing costs, making these systems more economically attractive.
* Market Awareness: A key challenge is a lack of awareness among consumers and businesses about the economic benefits of solar thermal systems. Increased consumer education can drive market adoption and, consequently, its contribution to the economy.

In summary, while the direct contribution of solar thermal technology to India's GDP is not as high as that of the IT sector or solar PV, its indirect impacts—through energy savings, reduced imports, job creation, and enhanced industrial competitiveness—are significant and growing. Its full potential is yet to be realized, and it is a key component of India's long-term strategy for energy security and a sustainable economy.

References:

1. Repsol ; www.repsol.com
2. EIA:www.eia.gov
3. Department of Energy: www.energy.gov
4. Sunrun:www.sunrun.com
5. ELPAIS : www.english.elpais.com
6. Diversegy: www.diversegy.com
7. wattco:www.wattco.com
8. SEIA:www.seia.org
9. Palmetto:www.solar.patmetto.gov
10. U.S.Envernomental:www.epa.com
11. Eco Flow: www.ecoflow.com

CHAPTER 6

WIND ENERGY IN INDIA, TECHNOLOGIES AND THEIR TECHNO-ECONOMIC ANALYSIS

INTRODUCTION

India has emerged as a significant player in the global wind energy sector, demonstrating strong commitment and making substantial progress towards its ambitious renewable targets.of 500 GW of non-fossil capacity by 2030. India continues to hold the fourth position globally in term of installed power capacity after China and Germany,position in global renewable energy capacity. The country's commitment to increase its share of solar and wind energy is evident through various initiatives and investments in green technology. This push not only aims to reduce carbon emissions but also to create a sustainable energy framework that supports economic growth and energy secure

MAIN FEATURES

India's recent policies encourage both public and private sectors to invest in clean energy projects, promoting innovation and job creation in the renewable sector. Additionally, international collaborations are being pursued to enhance technology transfer and grid integration. Continued efforts in research and development will further strengthen India's position in the global renewable energy landscape, fostering a cleaner, greener future for all.

private sector participation, attracting substantial foreign investment that supports infrastructure development. Furthermore, India's vast geographical diversity allows for significant potential in harnessing wind energy, particularly along its long coastline and in the interior regions where wind patterns are favorable.

The government has introduced various schemes to facilitate the growth of this sector, including enhanced grid connectivity for renewable sources and streamlined approval processes for projects. By fostering innovation in wind turbine technology and promoting local manufacturing, India is set to create jobs and stimulate economic activity within not just the energy sector, but across multiple industries reliant on sustainable energy sources.

* Growth: In the fiscal year 2024 This solidly positions India as the fourth largest in world in terms of wind capacity.
* Contribution As part of its dedication to climate action, India is also increasing its focus on financing for renewable energy initiatives, aiming to make green technologies more accessible. Partnerships with international organizations further bolster these efforts, ensuring that India remains at the forefront of the global renewable energy landscape. Through these combined efforts, India is not only addressing its energy needs but is also playing a crucial role in the worldwide transition towards a more sustainable future.
* Current Status and Capacity (A of March 31, 2025): Total installed wind power capacity reached 50 GW.

Energy Goals: Wind energy contributes significantly to the overall non-fossil fuel-based energy capacity, which has crossed 22.0 GW. India added 4.156 GW of new wind capacity, indicating a notable increase in installations.at 150m)

Gujaratat 120 meters above ground level

* 97.80 Gw at 15 *0 meters above ground level

India's recent policies actively encourage participation from both public and private sectors in clean energy ventures, fostering innovation and job creation within the renewable sector. Furthermore, international collaborations are being pursued to enhance technology transfer and facilitate grid integration. Continued investment in research and development will further solidify India's standing in the global renewable energy landscape, paving the way for a cleaner, greener future for all.

The engagement of the private sector has attracted substantial foreign investment that supports infrastructure development. Additionally, India's vast geographical diversity presents significant opportunities for harnessing wind energy, particularly along its extensive coastline and in interior regions where wind patterns are favorable. The government has instituted various schemes to promote the growth of this sector, including enhanced grid connectivity for renewable sources and streamlined approval processes for projects. By fostering innovation in wind turbine technology and advocating for local manufacturing, India is poised to create employment opportunities and stimulate economic activity not only within the energy sector but across multiple industries reliant on sustainable energy sources.

Growth: In the fiscal year 2024, this firmly positions India as the fourth largest nation in the world in terms of wind capacity.

Contribution: As part of its commitment to climate action, India is increasingly focusing on financing renewable energy initiatives, striving to make green technologies more accessible. Collaborations with international organizations further reinforce these endeavors, ensuring that India remains at the vanguard of the global renewable energy landscape. Through these combined efforts, India is not only addressing its energy requirements but is also playing a pivotal role in the global transition towards a more sustainable future.

Current Status and Capacity (As of March 31, 2025): Total installed wind power capacity has reached 50 GW. Wind energy significantly contributes to the overall non-fossil fuel-based energy capacity, which has surpassed 22.0 GW. India added 4.156 GW of new wind capacity, indicating a remarkable increase in installations at 150m above ground level.

Key Wind States: The majority of this potential is concentrated in eight states with significant wind resources, including Rajasthan (the highest potential), Maharashtra, Karnataka, Andhra Pradesh, and Tamil Nadu.

Wind Generation: Gujarat, Tamil Nadu, Karnataka, and Rajasthan lead in wind generation.

Installed Capacity: Gujarat has overtaken Tamil Nadu in installed capacity, securing the top position.

Wind Energy Capacity Potential: India possesses considerable wind energy potential, as indicated by recent assessments, with a gross wind power potential of 695.5 GW.

Future Projections: By 2030, India's installed wind power capacity is projected to reach 140 GW, reflecting a compound annual growth rate (CAGR) that underscores the nation's commitment to expanding its renewable portfolio.

Investment Forecast: Over the next five years, an estimated $20 billion is anticipated to be invested.

``` Installed Capacity: Guarat has surpassed Tamil Nadu in installed capacity, holding the top spot.

* Wind Energy Capacity Potential: India possesses substantial wind energy potential, according to recent assessments.

Gross Wind Power 695.5 Gw wind power potential

* Future Projections:
* By 2030, India's installed wind power capacity is projected to reach 140 GW, reflecting a compound annual growth rate (CAGR) that showcases the nation's commitment to expand its renewable portfolio.
```

* Investment Forecast: Over the next five years, an estimated $20 billion is expected to be invested in wind energy projects, which will enhance technological advancements and lower costs.

Policy Environment:

The government is set to implement new regulations to streamline project approvals further, ensuring a quicker transition from conception to execution. Local manufacturing incentives aim to reduce dependency on imported components, thus bolstering the domestic economy.

Community Involvement:

Initiatives to educate communities about the benefits of wind energy are gaining momentum, promoting local acceptance and support for wind projects.

Job training p

Programs are being launched to equip the workforce with the necessary skills to thrive in the renewable energy sector.

Technological Innovations: Advancements in smart grid technology and energy storage systems are anticipated to improve the efficiency and reliability of wind energy integration into the existing power infrastructure.

Research into new turbine designs is underway, focusing on enhancing energy capture efficiency and minimizing environmental impacts.

International Collaboration:

Bilateral partnerships with countries leading in wind technology offer opportunities for knowledge exchange and capacity building, which are critical for India's sustained growth in this sector.

Participation in global renewable energy forums further elevates India's stance, enabling the country to contribute to and learn from worldwide best practices in wind energy development.

India has significant of shore 85% wind energy potential particularly along the coastlines of Gujarat

Tamilnadu,and Karnataka

Almost at around 70(current potential capacity)

* Policies and Initiatives:
* "National Wind Solar Hybrid Policy (2018) Promotes Grid-connected wind solar PV hybrid system for optimal resources utilisation."
* "Resources Assessment:"

, National Institute of Wind Energy (NIWE) uses studies numbers wind energy"

* Funding/Schemes:
* "Green Venture Gap Funding (VGF) Scheme" "Approved & Signing VGF Scheme "till 2023 with 30 GW"

India's offshore Wind Energy project of P1 GW Tamil Nadu (courses) along with faculty for port upgradation." This suggests an offshore wind project in Tamil Nadu.

Please enter a normal meaningful text.

* Second Point: "Government policies and initiatives. The Indian government has been fostering wind energy growth through various sup policies." This is a general statement about government support for wind energy.
* Third Point: "Ambitious target is committed to achieve 500 GW of non-fossil fuel energy capacity by 2030, in which wind energy plays a crucial role. The GoI aims to add approximately 50 GW of renewable energy annually from FY 2023-24 to FY 2027-28." This highlights India's ambitious renewable energy targets, with wind energy being a significant contributor.
* Fourth Point: "Inter-State Transmission System (ISTS) Charges Waiver. This waiver for wind power projects commissioned by June 30, 2025 significantly reduces the cost of transmitting wind power across states, boosting its viability." This points to a specific policy (ISTS Charges Waiver) aimed at making wind energy more economically viable by reducing transmission costs.

- Reception

- Receive signals clearly and without interruptions

- Utilize advanced equipment for improved detection

- Analysis

- Decode messages accurately to extract valuable information

- Employ data validation methods to ensure reliability

- Security

- Implement encryption protocols to safeguard transmissions

- Regularly update systems to protect against vulnerabilities

- Collect input from users to enhance transmission standards

- Continuously monitor performance metrics for optimization

* Fifth Point: "National Wind-Solar Hybrid Policy (2018) promotes effective and best utilization and grid stability by encouraging the development of large wind connectivity to a solar hybrid system." This refers to the National Wind-Solar Hybrid Policy, emphasizing the integration of wind and solar for better grid stability and resource utilization.
* Sixth Point: "National Offshore Wind Energy Policy (2015) Aims to unlock the vast offshore wind potential. The union cabinet has approved a viability gap funding (VGF) scheme for 16W offshore wind projects (500MW each at Gujarat and Tamil Nadu coasts)." This mentions the National Offshore Wind Energy Policy and the approval of a Viability Gap Funding scheme for offshore wind projects in Gujarat and Tamil Nadu.

undercutting Stimulus through the Segment:

* Statement.
* Policy Framework of Wind Power.
* Repowering: Encourage replacing older, less efficient turbines with newer, higher capacity ones and optimize generation from existing sites.o
* Reinforce.Attract Private Sector Investment:
* Renewable Energy Targets: India has an ambitious target of achieving 500 GW of installed electric capacity from non-fossil sources by 2030, with 140 GW specifically from wind power.

- Types of Energy

- Kinetic Energy: Energy of motion, for example, in moving vehicles or flowing water

- Potential

* Fiscal Incentives: These include acceleration appreciation benefits, concessional customs on certain components, and 100% Foreign Direct Investment (FDI) under the automatic route.
* Incentives t Energy: Stored energy based on an object's position, such as a rock on a hill

- Energy Sources

- Renewable Energy: Harnessing natural processes, like solar, wind, and hydroelectric power

- Non-renewable Energy: Fossil fuels such as coal, oil, and natural gas that deplete over time

- Energy Conservation

- Utilize energy-efficient appliances to reduce consumption

- Implement habits such as turning off lights and unplugging devices when not in use

- Energy in Nutrition

- Understand the role of macronutrients: carbohydrates, proteins, and fats in providing energy

- Consider timing meals and snacks to maintain optimal energy levels throughout the day

* Fiscal and Financial Incentives:
* Accelerated Depreciation Benefit: Allows projects to declare a significant portion of wind power equipment value in past years.
* Concessional Customs Duty Exemption: On certain components of wind electric generators.
* Viability Gap Funding (VGF) Scheme: Approved for offshore wind energy projects to reduce the cost of power and make them viable.
* Interest Rate Rebates: For new wind energy projects and repowering initiatives.
* Policy Frameworks:
* National Wind-Solar Hybrid Policy 2018:
* Aims to promote large grid-connected wind.

Solar PV Hybrid System for Island Resources Ultra (likely "Ultra-Low" or "Ultra-High")

* National Offshore Wind Energy Policy 2015 (likely "2015")
* Subject is Vast Offshore Wind Energy Potential along India's Coastline, particularly Gujarat and Tamil Nadu.
* Guidelines for Tariff-Based Competitive Bidding Process for power from grid-connected or private transmission lines
* es. Waiver of Inter-State Transmission System (ISTS) charges for solar and wind power projects commissioned by June 30, 2025.
* Green Energy Corridor Project: For integrating renewable energy into the grid.
* Technical Support provided by the National Institute of Wind Energy (NIWE) for wind resource assessment and site identification.
* Financial Schemes:
* Pay the Indian Renewable Energy Development Agency (IREDA)
* Future Outlook:
* Indian states are planning to construct over 116 GW of grid capacity by 2030, indicating a strong future for wind energy.
* There is a growing focus on offshore wind energy with significant potential identified, especially off the coasts of Gujarat and Tamil Nadu.

India's aim to become a global exporter in wind manufacturing, its current annual manufacturing capacity, and the importance of renewable energy for a "robust grow

Potential Growth

- Set clear, achievable goals to enhance skills and knowledge - Reflect regularly on progress and adjust strategies as necessary

- Professional Growth - Seek opportunities for learning and development within your field

- Network with peers and mentors to gain new perspectives

- Emotional Growth

- Cultivate resilience by embracing challenges as learning experiences

- Practice gratitude to foster a positive mindset and outlook on life

- Spiritual Growth

- Explore beliefs and values through introspection and conversation

- Engage in practices that promote a sense of inner peace and purpose, such as yoga or meditation.

Wind Energy technology

technology-to harnesses the kinetic energy of wind and converts it into electricity. This renewable source of energy plays a crucial role in reducing reliance on fossil fuels and mitigating climate change.

* Breakdown of how it works different types and recent advancements:

Fundamental Principle

* Wind Capture: Wind turns the propeller - like blades of wind turbine.
* Rotor Rotation: - The blades are connected to rotor which then spins.

aerated, transmitted, used by homes and businesses).

* Types of Wind Energy Technologies:
* Wind energy systems:

Categorized by location and turbine design.

* Onshore Wind Energy:
* Turbines are installed in Generator: The spinning rotor connects to a generator (either directly or through a gearbox that speeds up RPM). The generator install and maintain due to harsh marine environments.
* Turbine types based on Fixed Bottom fOfshore Wind Turbines are

Referred directly to the sea floor in shallowerwaters (typically upto 60 meters deep).

* Floating offshore Wind: A newer technology where turbines are mounted on huge platforms anchored converts the mechanical energy from the spinning rotor into electrical energy through electromagnetic induction.
* Electricity: Its purpose (genlarge, open, rural, or mountainous areas with consistent wind flow.
* Generally more cost-eff**ective to install and widely deployed due to easier accessibility.**
* Challenges include visual impact, noise concerns, and land use.
* Offshore Wind Energy:
* Turbines are installed in bodies of water (oceans, large lakes).
* Benefits from stronger and more consistent winds over water, leading to higher energy production.
* Often involve longer turbines than onshore ones due to fewer transportation and infrastructure constraints.
* More expensive too sea floor with mooring lines.

This allows deployment in deep sea locations (greater than 60 meters) where wind resources are often even stronger.

Distributed Wind Energy:

* Smaller wind turbines installed close **to the end-user (e.g.** farms, small businesses, residences) to offset part of their energy needs.

Horizontal axis Wind Turbines (HAWTs):

The most common type, resembling traditional windmills rotating on axis facing into the wind

* Vertical Axis Wind Turbines (VAWTs):

Blades rotate around a vertical axis. They can capture wind from any direction without to you and can be more suitable for urban environments or specific low-wind conditions. Examples include Savonius and Darrieus Turbines.

Adancements and Future Trends

The Wind Energy Sector is constantly evolving with significant technological innovations.

* Larger and More Efficient Turbines:
* Manufacturers are developing increasingly large turbines with larger blade sizes for higher capacities. This allows for greater energy capture, reducing cost per megawatt-hour produced and improving economic viability.
* Especially for offshore wind farms.
* Advancements in materials (e.g., carbon fiber composites) are crucial for building high-strength, massive, durable, and lightweight blades.

* Floating Wind Farms:
* This is a major area of development.
* Enabling wind energy production in deep-water areas previously inaccessible to fixed-bottom turbines.
* Countries like Norway, Japan, and USA are pioneering this technology.
* AI and Data Analytics:
* Artificial Intelligence (AI) and Machine Learning (ML) are being used to predict wind patterns, optimize turbine operations, and maximize energy output.

Advanced sensors and monitoring": This describes how systems generate vast amounts of data, which analysts use for predictive maintenance, reducing downtime, and increasing turbine use.
* «Hydropower energy systems».

Techno-Economic Analysis (TEA) of wind energy technology is crucial for understanding its viability, competitiveness, and potential for future development. It involves a detailed assessment of both the technical performance and the associated economic costs throughout the wind farm's lifecycle.

Here's a breakdown of what a TEA for wind energy typically entails:

I. Technical Parameters:

* Site Assessment and Wind Resource Analysis:
* Wind Speed and Direction: Detailed measurements (e.g., using anemometers, LiDAR) at various heights to determine the average wind speed, wind shear, and turbulence. This is critical as energy output is proportional to the cube of wind speed (P \propto V^3).
* Wind Rose: Graphical representation of wind direction and speed distribution.
* Terrain and Obstacles: Impact of topography, buildings, and other obstacles on wind flow.
* Wake Effects: Energy losses due to turbines casting «wind shadows» on downwind turbines in a wind farm.
* Turbine Selection and Performance:
* Rated Power (MW): Maximum electrical output of the turbine.
* Rotor Diameter and Hub Height: Larger rotors capture more wind; higher hub heights access stronger, more consistent winds.
* Power Curve: A graph showing the electrical power output at different wind speeds.
* Capacity Factor (CF): The ratio of actual energy produced over a period to the maximum possible energy that could have been produced if the turbine operated at its rated power continuously. This is a key technical metric directly impacting revenue.
* Availability: Percentage of time the turbine is operational and ready to generate power.

* Technology Type: Direct-drive vs. geared, permanent magnet vs. electromagnet, etc., each with different efficiencies and maintenance requirements.
* Balance of Plant (BOP) Design:
* Foundations: Type and cost depend on soil conditions (onshore) or water depth and seabed conditions (offshore).
* Electrical Infrastructure: Collection system (cables between turbines), substation, and grid connection (transmission lines to the grid).
* Roads and Access: For construction and maintenance (onshore).
* Port Infrastructure: For offshore wind farms.

II. Economic Parameters and Cost Components:

* Capital Expenditure (CAPEX):
* Turbine Cost: Typically the largest component, varying significantly with size (MW), manufacturer, and technology. (e.g., commercial 3.5 MW turbines can cost upwards of £3.13 million, with offshore turbines being significantly more expensive per MW).
* Foundations: Civil works, materials, and installation.
* Electrical Infrastructure: Cables, transformers, switchgear, substation, grid connection fees.
* Site Preparation and Roads: Clearing, leveling, and road construction.
* Assembly and Installation: Cranes, specialized crews, logistics.
* Consulting and Permitting: Feasibility studies, environmental impact assessments, legal fees, permits.
* Land Acquisition/Lease: Cost of land for onshore wind farms or lease of seabed for offshore.
* Contingency: An allowance for unforeseen costs.
* Operational Expenditure (OPEX):
* Operations and Maintenance (O&M):
* Scheduled Maintenance: Routine inspections, lubrication, component replacements.
* Unscheduled Maintenance/Repairs: Costs associated with breakdowns, spare parts, and specialized repairs. Offshore wind typically has higher O&M costs due to logistical challenges.
* Labor Costs: Technicians, operators, administrative staff.
* Service Contracts: Often provided by turbine manufacturers.
* Insurance: Property, liability, and business interruption insurance.
* Lease Payments/Taxes: Land lease payments, property taxes.
* Grid Connection Fees: Ongoing charges for using the transmission network.
* Downtime Costs: Lost revenue due to turbine unavailability.
* Revenue Streams:

* Electricity Sales: Price per MWh sold to the grid (e.g., via Power Purchase Agreements (PPAs), spot market). This is highly dependent on market prices, regulatory frameworks (e.g., feed-in tariffs), and renewable energy certificates (RECs).
* Capacity Payments (if applicable): Payments for providing available capacity to the grid.

III. Financial Metrics and Analysis:

* Levelized Cost of Energy (LCOE):
* This is arguably the most critical metric. LCOE represents the average lifetime cost of electricity generation, expressed in currency per unit of energy (e.g., $/MWh, ₹/kWh).
* It accounts for all CAPEX, OPEX, financing costs, and energy production over the project›s lifetime, discounted to a net present value.
* Formula: LCOE = (Sum of all discounted costs over lifetime) / (Sum of all discounted energy produced over lifetime).
* Significance: Enables direct comparison of the cost-competitiveness of wind energy with other generation technologies (solar, fossil fuels, nuclear). Wind LCOE has significantly decreased over the past decade, making it one of the cheapest forms of new electricity generation in many regions.
* Net Present Value (NPV):
* Calculates the present value of all cash inflows minus the present value of all cash outflows over the project›s life. A positive NPV indicates a financially attractive project.
* Internal Rate of Return (IRR)
* The discount rate at which the NPV of all cash flows from a particular project equals zero. A higher IRR indicates a more desirable project.
* Payback Period:
* The time it takes for the cumulative cash inflows to equal the initial investment.
* Sensitivity Analysis:
* Examining how changes in key variables (e.g., wind speed, capacity factor, turbine price, O&M costs, electricity price, discount rate) impact the LCOE and other financial metrics. This helps identify the most influential factors and project risks.
* Risk Assessment:
* Resource Risk: Uncertainty in wind resource assessment.
* Technology Risk: Performance, reliability, and lifespan of turbines.
* Market Risk: Fluctuations in electricity prices, changes in policy.
* Regulatory Risk: Changes in subsidies, permitting processes.
* Financing Risk: Interest rates, availability of capital.

Key Trends and Factors Influencing Wind TEA

* Technology Advancements: Larger turbines, higher hub heights, improved aerodynamics, and more efficient generators continue to drive down LCOE by increasing energy capture and reducing per-MWh costs.
* Economies of Scale: Larger wind farms benefit from reduced per-MW costs in terms of installation, infrastructure, and O&M.
* Supply Chain Development: Maturation of the wind industry supply chain leads to reduced component costs and improved logistics.
* Offshore Wind: While typically having higher CAPEX and OPEX than onshore, offshore wind benefits from stronger, more consistent wind resources and less land-use constraint. Floating offshore wind is an emerging technology with specific techno-economic considerations.
* Government Policies and Incentives: Subsidies, tax credits, renewable energy mandates, and favorable grid connection policies significantly impact project economics.
* Grid Integration Costs: The intermittent nature of wind power necessitates grid upgrades, balancing services, and potentially energy storage, which can add to the overall system cost.

A comprehensive TEA for wind energy provides a robust framework for investors, policymakers, and developers to make informed decisions regarding the deployment and optimization of wind power projects, accelerating the transition to a sustainable energy future.

CONCLUSION

As part of its commitment to climate action, India is increasingly focusing on financing renewable energy initiatives, striving to make green technologies more accessible. Collaborations with international organizations further reinforce these endeavors, ensuring that India remains at the vanguard of the global renewable energy landscape. Through these combined efforts, India is not only addressing its energy requirements but is also playing a pivotal role in the global transition towards a more sustainable future.

References

1. MNRE Annual Reports 2021-22, 2022-23 23-24 2024-25`.
2. Global Wind Energy Council - www.gwec.net"
3. CEEW - www.ceew.in"
4. Ember - ember-energy.org"
5. ReseargGate - www.researchgate.net"
6. Ministry of Power - powermin.gov.in"
7. DAAD - German Academic Exchange..."
8. Dr. Sinay - Sinay.ai"

9. Smith Gregyuan-a.org"
10. National Grid (www.nationalgrid.com)
11. NREL (www.nrel.gov)
12. The America clean Power (cleanpower.org)
13. University of Plymouth (www.plymouth.ac.uk
14. IEA - International Energy (www.iea.org)
15. Department of Energy (www.energy.gov)
16. Porsche Energy (www.porscheenergy.com) -

CHAPTER 7

BIOMASS ENERGY, TECHNOLOGIES, THEIR TECHNO-ECONOMIC ANALYSIS AND CONTRIBUTION OF BIOMASS ENERGY TO NATIONAL GDP

Abstract

- **Biomass energy plays a significant role in India's energy landscape, particularly in rural areas, and is a key component of the country's renewable energy strategy.India's bioeconomy grew from $10 billion in 2014 to $165.7 billion in 2024, with a target of $300 billion by 2030.The sector contributes 4.25% to India's GDP and has demonstrated a compound annual growth rate (CAGR) of 17.9% over the past four years.**

Introduction

India has a substantial biomass potential, with an estimated 750 million metric tonnes (MMT) of biomass available annually, and a surplus of about 230 MMT/year. This primarily comes from agricultural residues, municipal solid waste, animal waste, and forestry residues.

: Biomass currently accounts for approximately 32% of India's total primary energy use.

Over 70% of Indians depend on biomass for their energy needs across the value chain, especially in households.

- **Installed Capacity:** As of August 2022, over 800 biomass power projects, bagasse cogeneration, and non- bagasse cogeneration projects have been installed, with an aggregated capacity of 10,632 MW for power generation and 140 TPD for compressed biogas (CBG) production.
- **Co-firing in Thermal Power Plants:** To reduce air pollution from stubble burning and decarbonize power generation, India has mandated co-firing of biomass along with coal in thermal power plants. This started with a minimum 5% co-firing from FY 2024-25, increasing to 7% from FY 2025-26.

- **Biofuels:** India is pushing for increased blending of biofuels, with targets of 20% ethanol blending by 2025/26, 5% biodiesel blending by 2030, and 5% CBG blending by 2028/29.

Government Policies and Initiatives: The Ministry of New and Renewable Energy (MNRE) is the primary body promoting biomass energy in India. Key policies and programs include:

- **National Bioenergy Programme (NBP):** Continued till 2025-2026 with a substantial budget outlay, this program aims to promote energy recovery from biomass.
- **National Policy on Biofuels:** Aims for significant blending targets of biofuels with fossil fuels.
- **Waste to Energy Programme (WTEP):** Focuses on converting agro-industrial waste into energy, offering capital subsidies for biomass pellet plants and financial support for compressed biogas (CBG) projects.
- **Renewable Energy Investment Promotion Policy (REIPP):** Encourages foreign direct investment (FDI) in the biomass sector, offers reduced GST on biomass equipment, and provides infrastructure support.
- **Pradhan Mantri JI-VAN (Jaiv Indhan - Vatavaran Anukool Fasal Awashesh Nivaran) Yojana:** Provides financial support for integrated bio-ethanol projects, particularly for advanced biofuel projects using lignocellulosic biomass.
- **Fiscal and Tax Incentives:** Includes accelerated depreciation, GST benefits, and eligibility for carbon credits.
- **National Biomass Repository:** MNRE plans to create a nationwide appraisal program to ensure the availability of biofuels from domestic feedstock.

Challenges:

Despite its immense potential, biomass energy in India faces several challenges:

- **Supply Chain Management:** Ensuring a consistent and reliable supply of biomass feedstock is difficult due to seasonal variations, logistical issues, and competition with other uses of biomass.
- **Technological Barriers:** There's a need for continuous innovation and investment in efficient biomass conversion processes and advanced technologies.
- **Financial Constraints:** High initial capital costs and limited access to financing are major hurdles, despite government incentives.
- **Regulatory Issues:** The biomass industry is subject to complex and sometimes cumbersome regulatory frameworks.
- **Quality and Storage:** Maintaining biomass quality (e.g., moisture content) and proper storage are crucial for efficient plant operation.

- **Competition for Feedstock:** Pellet suppliers often prefer selling to other industries (textile, food processing) at higher prices than to thermal power plants, leading to supply shortages for co-firing.
- **Environmental Concerns:** While generally considered carbon-neutral, burning certain biomass can cause pollution, and some processes can increase methane emissions if not properly managed.

Biomass technology refers to the various processes and systems that convert biomass into useful forms of energy (heat, electricity, fuels) or other valuable products.

What is Biomass?

In the context of energy, biomass is organic material that comes from recently living plants and animals. It's a renewable resource because plants can be regrown and animal waste is continuously produced. Common examples of biomass include:

* **Wood and wood waste:** Firewood, wood pellets, wood chips, sawdust from lumber mills, black liquor from pulp and paper mills.

  Agricultural crops and waste: Corn, soybeans, sugarcane, switchgrass, algae, crop residues (like corn stover or wheat straw), and food processing residues.
* **Biogenic materials in municipal solid waste (MSW):** Paper products, cotton, wool, food waste, yard waste.

  Animal manure and human sewage: Used to produce biogas.

How Biomass is Converted to Energy

(Biomass technology):

Biomass is converted into energy through several methods, broadly categorized as:

Direct Combustion (Burning): This is the most common and simplest method. Biomass is directly burned to produce heat, which can be used for:

Heating buildings and water.

- Industrial process heat.
- **Generating electricity**
- Thermochemical **Conversion:** These processes involve heating biomass at high temperatures in control
- **Pyrolysis**: Heating biomass in the absence of oxygen to produce bio-oil (a liquid fuel), syngas (a gas mixture of hydrogen and carbon monoxide), and biochar (a solid carbon-rich material).

- **Gasification:** Heating biomass with a controlled amount of oxygen and/or steam at high temperatures (over 700°C) to convert it into**Syngas** can then be used to generate electricity or as a precursor for other chemical processes.
- **Torrefaction:** Heating biomass at lower temperatures (200-300°C) without oxygen to remove moisture and volatile compounds, resulting in a "bio-coal" or "biochar" that is denser and more energy-rich.
- **Hydrothermal Conversion** (e.g., Hydrothermal Liquefaction - HTL, Hydrothermal Gasification - HTG, Hydrothermal Carbonization -

HTC): These methods use water, high temperatures, and pressure to break down biomass, often effective for wet biomass. They can produce bio-oil, syngas, or hydrochar.

* **Biochemical Conversion:** These processes use microorganisms to break down biomass.
- **Anaerobic Digestion**: Organic matter is broken down by bacteria in the absence of oxygen to produce biogas (primarily methane), which can be used for heat or electricity. This is commonly used for animal manure and sewage.
- **Fermentation:** Sugars from biomass are converted into ethanol (a liquid biofuel) by yeast or bacteria. This is commonly used for crops like corn and sugarcane. Applications of Biomass Technology:
* **Electricity Generation (Biopower):** Biomass power plants burn biomass or use gasification/ anaerobic digestion to generate electricity, either for direct use or to feed into the grid.
* **Heat Generation:** Biomass boilers and furnaces provide heat for residential, commercial, and industrial purposes.
* **Combined Heat and Power (CHP)**: Systems that simultaneously produce both heat and electricity from biomass, increasing overall energy efficiency.
* **Biofuels Production**: Converting biomass into liquid or gaseous fuels like biodiesel, bioethanol, biogas, and biohydrogen fortransportation.
* **Bioproducts:** Biomass can be converted into chemicals for making plastics and other products that are typically derived from fossil fuels.
* **Biochar Production:** Biochar, a product of pyrolysis, can be used for soil improvement, carbon sequestration, and **bioremediation.** Advantages of Biomass Technology:
* **Renewable Resource:** Biomass is constantly replenished as plants grow and waste is generated.
* **Waste Reduction:** It utilizes organic waste materials (agricultural residues, forestry waste, municipal solid waste) that would otherwise go to landfills.
* **Carbon Neutral Potential**: While burning biomass releases CO2, the plants from which it originated absorb CO2 during their growth,creating a potentially balanced carbon cycle if managed sustainably.

* **Reliable and Dispatchable**: Unlike solar and wind, biomass power plants can operate continuously and produce electricity on demand, providing a stable energy source.
* **Job Creation:** The biomass industry supports jobs in cultivation, harvesting, processing, and plant operation.
* **Decentralized Energy**: Can be used in off-grid or remote areas where centralized energy infrastructure is limited.

Disadvantages of Biomass Technology:

* **Land Use and Deforestation**: Large-scale cultivation of energy crops can compete with food production and contribute to deforestation if not managed sustainably.
* **Air Pollution:** Burning biomass can release pollutants like carbon monoxide, nitrogen oxides, and particulate matter, similar to fossil fuels, if not properly controlled.
* **Resource Intensive**: Production, transportation, and utilization of biomass can require significant amounts of water, fertilizers, and energy, potentially offsetting some environmental benefits.
* **Efficiency**: Some biomass fuels, like ethanol, may be less efficient than traditional fossil fuels.
* **High Costs:** The initial investment for biomass conversion technologies can be substantial.
* **Transportation Challenges**: Biomass often has a lower energy density than fossil fuels, making transportation over long distances less economical.

Sustainability Concerns: The "carbon neutrality" of biomass is debated and depends heavily on sustainable harvesting practices and efficient conversion technologies to ensure that Biomass technology refers to the various processes and systems that convert biomass into useful forms of energy (heat, electricity, fuels) or other valuable products.

In the context of energy, biomass is organic material that comes from recently living plants and animals. It's a renewable resource because plants can be regrown and animal waste is continuously produced. Common examples of biomass include:

* **Wood and wood waste**: Firewood, wood pellets, wood chips, sawdust from lumber mills, black liquor from pulp and paper mills.
* **Agricultural crops and waste: Corn**, soybeans, sugarcane, switchgrass, algae, crop residues (like corn stover or wheat straw), and food processing residues.
* **Biogenic materials in municipal solid waste (MSW)**: Paper products, cotton, wool, food waste, yard waste.
* **Animal manure and human sewage:** Used to produce biogas. How Biomass is Converted to Biomass is converted into energy through several methods, broadly categorized as:
* **Direct Combustion (Burning):** This is the most common and simplest method. Biomass is directly burned to produce heat, which can be used for:

- Heating buildings and water.
- Industrial process heat.
- **Generating electricity in steam turbines.**

* **Thermochemical Conversion**: These processes involve heating biomass at high temperatures in controlled environments.

- **Pyrolysis:** Heating biomass in the absence of oxygen to produce bio-oil (a liquid fuel), syngas (a gas mixture of hydrogen and carbon monoxide), and biochar (a solid carbon-rich material).
- **Gasification:** Heating biomass with a controlled amount of oxygen and/or steam at high temperatures (over 700°C) to convert it into

Syngas can then be used to generate electricity or as a precursor for other chemical processes.

- **Torrefaction**: Heating biomass at lower temperatures (200-300°C) without oxygen to remove moisture and volatile compounds, resulting in a "bio-coal" or "biochar" that is denser and more energy-rich.
- Hydrothermal Conversion (e.g., Hydrothermal Liquefaction - HTL, Hydrothermal Gasification - HTG, Hydrothermal Carbonization -

HTC): These methods use water, high temperatures, and pressure to break down biomass, often effective for wet biomass. They can produce bio-oil, syngas, or hydrochar.

* **Biochemical Conversion:** These processes use microorganisms to break down biomass.

- Anaerobic Digestion: Organic matter is broken down by bacteria in the absence of oxygen to produce biogas (primarily methane), which can be used for heat or electricity. This is commonly used for animal manure and sewage.
- **Fermentation:** Sugars from biomass are converted into ethanol (a liquid biofuel) by yeast or bacteria. This is commonly used for cropslike corn and sugarcane. Applications of Biomass Technology:

* **Electricity Generation (Biopower)**: Biomass power plants burn biomass or use gasification/ anaerobic digestion to generate electricity, either for direct use or to feed into the grid.

* Heat Generation: Biomass boilers and furnaces provide heat for residential, commercial, and industrial purposes.

* **Combined Heat and Power (CHP):** Systems that simultaneously produce both heat and electricity from biomass, increasing overall energy efficiency.

* **Biofuels Production:** Converting biomass into liquid or gaseous fuels like biodiesel, bioethanol, biogas, and biohydrogen for transportation.

* **Bioproducts**: Biomass can be converted into chemicals for making plastics and other products that are typically derived from fossil fuels.

* water, fertilizers, and energy, potentially offsetting some environmental benefits.

* **Efficiency**: Some biomass fuels, like ethanol, may be less efficient than traditional fossil fuels.
* **High Costs**: The initial investment for biomass conversion technologies can be substantial.

In the context of energy, biomass is organic material that comes from recently living plants and animals. It's a renewable resource because plants can be regrown and animal waste is continuously produced. Common examples of biomass include:

* Wood and wood waste: Firewood, wood pellets, wood chips, sawdust from lumber mills, black liquor from pulp and paper mills.
* **Agricultural crops and waste:** Corn, soybeans, sugarcane, switchgrass, algae, crop residues (like corn stover or wheat straw), and food processing residues.
* **Biogenic materials in municipal solid waste (MSW):** Paper products, cotton, wool, food waste, yard waste.

  manure and human sewage: Used to produce biogas. How Biomass is Converted to **Energy (Biomass Technology)**:

Biomass is converted into energy through several methods, broadly categorized as:

* Direct Combustion (Burning): This is the most common and simplest method. Biomass is directly burned to produce heat, which can be used for:

- Heating buildings and water.
* Industrial process heat..

Techno-Economic Analysis (TEA) is a comprehensive evaluation method that combines technical and economic assessments of an industrial process, product, or service. It's used to determine the economic performance and feasibility of a technology, especially emerging ones, by linking technical parameters to financial metrics.

Here's a breakdown of what a TEA entails:

Purpose of a Techno-Economic Analysis:

- **Go/No-Go Decisions:** Helps in making informed decisions about whether to pursue research, development, and investment in a particular technology or project.
- **Economic Feasibility:** Assesses if a process will be profitable under various assumptions, helping companies avoid pursuing dead ends.
- **Risk Mitigation:** Identifies potential bottlenecks and risks, allowing for the development of contingency plans.
- **Optimization:** Helps prioritize research efforts and identify areas for process optimization and cost reduction.

- **Benchmarking:** Compares an emerging technology's technical and commercial performance against existing commercial benchmarks.
- **Investment Decisions:** Provides a clear picture of the economic impact for investors and entrepreneurs.

Key Components of a Techno-Economic Analysis:

* **Technical Assessment:**

- **Process Design & Modeling:** Defining the system with a process flow diagram (PFD), material and energy balances, operating conditions (temperature, pressure, flow rates), and efficiencies.
- **Equipment Sizing:** Estimating the size and utility requirements for each piece of equipment.
- **Technology Maturity:** Evaluating the readiness level and appropriateness of the technology.

* **Economic Evaluation:**

- **Capital Expenditures (CAPEX):** Costs associated with building, machinery, reactors, equipment, installation, land, etc.
- **Operational Expenditures (OPEX):** Ongoing costs like electricity, water, raw materials, labor, maintenance, rent, etc.
- **Revenue Projections:** Estimating potential income from the product or service.
- **Financial Metrics:** Calculating key indicators such as:
- **Net Present Value (NPV):** The difference between the present value of cash inflows and the present value of cash outflows over a period of time.
- **Internal Rate of Return (IRR):** The discount rate at which the NPV of all cash flows from a project equals zero.
- **Payback Period:** The time it takes for the initial investment to be recovered from net cash inflows.
- **Return on Investment (ROI):** A ratio that evaluates the profitability of an investment.
- **Minimum Selling Price (MSP):** The lowest price at which a product can be sold to cover all costs and achieve a desired return.

* **Sensitivity Analysis:**

- Evaluating how changes in key technical or economic parameters (e.g., raw material costs, energy prices, product yield) affect the overall economic outcomes. This helps identify the most critical variables and potential risks.

* **Risk Management:**

- Identifying potential risks and developing strategies to mitigate them.

Steps in Conducting a Techno-Economic Analysis:

While the exact steps can vary, a general approach includes:

5. **Define Goal and Scope:** Clearly articulate the project's objectives, boundaries, and the specific questions the TEA aims to answer.
6. **Develop a Technology Analysis Plan:** Create a roadmap outlining the approach, methodology, and a preliminary process flow diagram.
7. **Create a Performance Model:** Utilize engineering principles and software (if applicable) to model the process, including mass and energy balances, conversion rates, and equipment specifications.
8. **Cost Estimation:** Estimate both capital and operating costs based on the technical model, often using industry benchmarks and cost estimation methodologies (e.g., AACE International's estimate classes).
9. **Financial Analysis:** Calculate the relevant financial metrics (NPV, IRR, payback period, etc.) to assess the economic viability.
10. **Sensitivity and Risk Analysis:** Perform sensitivity analyses to understand the impact of uncertainties and identify key risks.
11. **Reporting:** Present the findings in a clear, transparent report, including assumptions, results, and an assessment of uncertainties and risks.

Applications of Techno-Economic Analysis:

TEA is widely used across various industries, particularly in:

- **Chemical and Bioprocess Industries:** Evaluating new production processes, biorefineries, and chemical syntheses.
- **Energy Sector:** Assessing the feasibility of renewable energy technologies (solar, wind, biofuels), power plants, and energy storage systems.
- **Petroleum Industry:** Analyzing new extraction and refining methods.
- **Waste-to-Energy:** Evaluating technologies for converting waste into valuable products or energy.
- **New Technology Development:** Guiding R&D, engineering, and business decisions throughout the technology development lifecycle.

Software and Tools for TEA:

Various software and tools can assist in conducting TEAs, ranging from specialized process simulation software to more general economic modeling tools:

- **Process Simulation Software:** Aspen Plus, Aspen Hysys ChemCAD
- SuperPro Designer (especially for bioprocesses)
- **Economic Analysis Tools (often integrated or standalone):**

- Microsoft Excel (for building custom models)
- NREL's System Advisor Model (SAM) (for renewable energy projects) NREL's REopt (for optimal mix of energy technologies)
- DIgSILENT's Economic Analysis Tools (for power network and plant developments)
- Specialized software suites developed by research institutions or companies (e.g., Techno Economics' TESS).

By combining technical rigor with financial analysis, TEA provides a robust framework for evaluating the potential of new technology

Contributes to a country's Gross Domestic Product (GDP)

through various direct and indirect economic activities. Here's a breakdown of how it makes a significant impact:

Direct Contributions:

1. **Investment in Infrastructure:**
    1. Construction of biomass power plants, biogas digesters, and biofuel refineries.
    2. Manufacturing and installation of equipment (boilers, turbines, anaerobic digesters, etc.).
    3. Development of biomass collection, storage, and processing facilities.

2. **Job Creation:**

1. **Direct Employment:** In biomass cultivation (e.g., dedicated energy crops), harvesting, transportation, processing, and operation and maintenance of biomass facilities.
2. **Research and Development:** Jobs in developing new biomass technologies and improving existing ones.

3. **Sale of Energy Products:**
    1. Revenue generated from selling electricity to the grid.
    2. Sale of heat for industrial or residential use.
    3. Production and sale of biofuels (ethanol, biodiesel) for transportation.
    4. Sale of biogas for various applications (cooking, power generation).

4. **Value-Added Products:**

1. Beyond energy, biomass can be used to produce bio-based chemicals, materials, and other valuable products, adding to the manufacturing sector's contribution to GDP.

Indirect and Induced Contributions:

1. Rural Economic Development:

1. Biomass feedstock production often occurs in rural areas, providing new income streams for farmers and foresters.
2. This can help reduce rural poverty and stimulate local economies.
3. Increased demand for agricultural inputs (fertilizers, equipment) and related services.

2. Reduced Fossil Fuel Imports:

1. For countries reliant on imported fossil fuels, biomass energy can decrease energy import bills, thereby improving the balance of trade and keeping more money within the domestic economy. This dollar saving indirectly boosts GDP.

3. Energy Security:

1. Utilizing indigenous biomass resources enhances national energy security, reducing vulnerability to volatile global energy markets. This stability fosters a more predictable economic environment for businesses and investors.

4. Technological Innovation:

1. Investment in biomass energy drives innovation in sustainable technologies, fostering a knowledge-based economy and creating new industries and businesses.

5. Environmental Benefits with Economic Value:

1. While not directly measured in GDP, the environmental benefits (reduced greenhouse gas emissions, improved waste management, better air quality) have economic value in terms of avoided costs (e.g., healthcare costs due to pollution, climate change adaptation costs). This contributes to a more sustainable long-term economic growth.

6. Multiplier Effect:

1. The direct spending in the biomass sector creates a ripple effect throughout the economy. For example, wages paid to biomass workers are then spent on goods and services, supporting other businesses (indirect effects). These businesses, in turn, create more jobs and income (induced effects).

India's Context:

India's bioeconomy, which includes biomass energy, has shown significant growth.

- India's bioeconomy grew from **$10 billion in 2014 to $165.7 billion in 2024**, with a target of **$300 billion by 2030**.
- The sector contributes **4.25% to India's GDP** and has demonstrated a compound annual growth rate (CAGR) of 17.9% over the past four years.
- Bioenergy specifically contributes to energy security, sustainability, and rural development. For instance, second-generation ethanol refineries converting agricultural residues into fuel strengthen the circular economy and reduce pollution.
- Government support and favorable policies are key drivers for the biomass market in India, with targets for renewable energy capacity including a significant portion from biomass.

Conclusiom

- **In essence, biomass energy, as part of the broader renewable energy and bioeconomy sectors, plays a multifaceted role in contributing to GDP by generating revenue, creating jobs, fostering innovation, enhancing energy security, and promoting rural development.**
- **Biomass energy plays a significant role in India's energy landscape, particularly in rural areas, and is a key component of the country's renewable energy strategy.India's bioeconomy grew from $10 billion in 2014 to $165.7 billion in 2024, with a target of $300 billion by 2030.The sector contributes 4.25% to India's GDP and has demonstrated a compound annual growth rate (CAGR) of 17.9% over the past four years.**

References

1. Annual Reports-2021-22,22-23,23-24,24-25
2. Energy Information www,eig,gov
3. Department of Energy www,energy,gov
4. Farm Energy form-energy.extension.org
5. Pyrolysis gasificationplant .com
6. SDA(gov) climatelinks.usda.gov

BIOGRAPHY

Graduated from Lucknow University with post-graduation and Ph.D. (Mathematics) from the same university. He has been always a "meritorious student."

After completing education, joined the Govt. of India through U.P.S.C. in the National Planning Commission(1985) and was involved in conceptualizing, formulating, and implementing the "National Programme, Integrated Rural Energy Programme(IREP)" in 780 blocks (one in each district) across the country.

Later, migrated to the Ministry of Non-Conventional Energy. Was responsible for consolidating and integrate IREP with other ongoing non-conventional energy programs for effective implementation.

Subsequently, joined "Prestigeous"Office of the Principle Scientifics Adviser to the Government of India (where he was responsible for evolving National Energy Map of India.) From there, in2010 retired from Govt service.

He was also responsible in Planning commission for establishing five IREP Training Centers, each in Delhi, Gujarat, UP (Lucknow), and Meghalaya (Shillong). These centers are functioning as "Centre of Excellence."